Differentiating Instruction for Students With Learning Disabilities

CORWIN
PRESS

The Corwin Press logo—a raven striding across an open book—represents the happy union of courage and learning. We are a professional-level publisher of books and journals for K–12 educators, and we are committed to creating and providing resources that embody these qualities. Corwin's motto is "Success for All Learners."

William N. Bender

Differentiating Instruction for Students With Learning Disabilities

Best Teaching
Practices
for
General
and
Special
Educators

CORWIN PRESS, INC.
A Sage Publications Company
Thousand Oaks, California

Council for
Exceptional
Children

For information:

Corwin Press, Inc.
A Sage Publications Company
2455 Teller Road
Thousand Oaks, California 91320
E-mail: www.corwinpress.com

Sage Publications Ltd.
6 Bonhill Street
London EC2A 4PU
United Kingdom

Sage Publications India Pvt. Ltd.
M-32 Market
Greater Kailash I
New Delhi 110 048 India

Printed in the United States of America

Library of Congress Cataloging-in-Publication Data

Bender, William N.
    Differentiating instruction for students with learning disabilities:
best teaching practices for general and special educators
    / William Bender.
        p. cm.
    Includes bibliographical references and index.
    ISBN 0-7619-4516-4 (c)
    ISBN 0-7619-4517-2 (p)
    1. Learning disabled children-Education. 2. Individualized
instruction. I. Title.
    LC4704.5 .B46 2002
    371.92'6-dc21   2002006452

This book is printed on acid-free paper.

02 03 04 05 10 9 8 7 6 5 4

Acquisitions Editor:	Robb Clouse
Editorial Assistant:	Erin Clow
Copy Editor:	Gillian Dickens
Production Editor:	Denise Santoyo
Cover Designer:	Michael Dubowe
Production Artist:	Janet Foulger
Typesetter:	Tina Hill
Indexer:	Kathy Paparchontis

Contents

About the Author

William Bender earned his Ph.D. from the University of North Carolina in 1983. Prior to this, he taught eighth- and ninth-grade students in the public school system for several years. Since he has been in higher education, he has published more than sixty research articles and nine books in special education and education. He specializes in instructional strategies and disciplinary strategies for students with disabilities, particularly learning disabilities, emotional disturbance, and attention disorders. He is recognized as a national leader on instructional tactics and distance education. His combination of practical strategies and easy humor leads to a demand for numerous workshops each year on various topics in education. He would like to receive your comments on this work and invites e-mail from both educators and parents nationwide at wnbender@coe.uga.edu.

Acknowledgments

The contributions of the following reviewers are gratefully acknowledged:

Deborah S. Yost
Chair, Department of Education
La Salle University
Philadelphia, PA

Judith Frank-Gonwa
Principal, Wescott School
Northbrook, IL

William A. Rieck
Professor, College of Education
University of Louisiana – Lafayette
Lafayette, LA

Merle Burbridge
Consulting Teacher, Hemet Unified School District
Hemet , CA

Theresa Sofianos
Teacher, Henking School
Glenview, IL

Kathleen McLane
Senior Director, Publications and Continuing Education
Council for Exceptional Children
Arlington, VA

Helen Johnston
Special Education Teacher, Calvert County Public Schools
Prince Frederick, MD

Mary Blake
Special Education Teacher, The Family School
New York City, NY

Introduction

Students with learning disabilities, as a group, are some of the most courageous students I have ever dealt with. I have taught students with learning disabilities, directly and indirectly, for more than twenty years and, although I have seen my share of behavioral problems from these students, it is wise to reflect for a moment on what the ultimate cause for those problems may be. These students are continually frustrated in their learning endeavors by the difficulty of the assignments given them, and misbehavior is often the result. Furthermore, students with learning disabilities may be ridiculed by their peers; they are often the victims of overt bias, ignorance, and outright hostility from peers (and, even in this day and age, from some teachers).

Still, most students with learning disabilities do not demonstrate highly disruptive behavior problems, and most generally manage to confront their particular disabilities, compensate for them in some fashion, and move forward with their learning and their lives in productive ways. I am always humbled when I begin a project such as this book, simply because of the continuous courage and dedication I see in the students that this book is ultimately designed to help. I sincerely hope that this text may make their learning somewhat easier and their lives a bit simpler.

Thus, the ultimate purpose of this text is to highlight a variety of differentiated instructional strategies (Gregory & Chapman, 2002; Tomlinson, 1999) that work for students with learning disabilities in the special education and the inclusive general education classroom. As educators, we all realize that most students with learning disabilities spend almost all of their school day in inclusive general education classes (Mastropieri & Scruggs, 1998), and consequently, teachers need differentiated instructional strategies that are proven to work for these students in those classrooms. Fortunately, research has proceeded over the past two decades, and we can now state fairly definitively that a number of instructional strategies will work for students with learning disabilities (Vaughn, Gersten, & Chard, 2000). Thus, the ideas presented here are, for the most part, research-proven ideas, and although not exhaustive, these strategies do represent the best practices to date for students with learning disabilities. Implementation of a variety of these strategies in the special education class or the inclusive class will focus the efforts of both teachers and students on academic success and will result in higher overall academic achievement for students with learning disabilities, as well as greater satisfaction in the class generally.

This book is not intended as an introduction to learning disabilities, and no information on characteristics of these students is presented, except as an explanation of why a particular tactic is effective. Also,

> Students with learning disabilities, as a group, are some of the most courageous students I have ever dealt with.

although this book includes some summaries of the latest research, this is not intended as a comprehensive research review. Furthermore, a number of these strategies have been explored over a longer period of time—self-monitoring is one example, and the research cited does include some of the initial and seminal references for this and other tactics. However, the major focus is not an exhaustive exposition of available research but rather a working knowledge of how and why these strategies are so strongly suggested for students with learning disabilities.

The differentiated instruction concept will serve as the primary model for this text, and the strategies described in each chapter will be presented within the context of that model (Gregory & Chapman, 2002; Tomlinson, 1999; Tomlinson et al., 2002). I have used the term *strategies* for effective, yet somewhat involved, instructional procedures, and I use the term *tactic* for quickly implemented instructional ideas. Furthermore, the content/process/product structure of the differentiated instructional concept will be explored for the instructional strategies that are recommended herein (Tomlinson, 1999), and thus the differentiated instructional construct will serve as a background for the entire text. Many reflective exercises for teachers will focus on relating the recommended strategies herein to the differentiated instructional model of teaching.

Chapter 1 presents the concept of differentiated instruction and how that concept translates into instruction for students with learning disabilities in the special education or the inclusive classroom. Chapter 2 involves the emerging insights into instruction stemming from the brain-compatible instruction literature—one foundation for the differentiated instructional construct. A seminal finding of the brain-compatible learning research is that learning must have meaning for students; furthermore, students must take personal responsibility for their own learning. Chapters 3 and 4 involve supporting students academically, using a variety of metacognitive and/or scaffolded learning techniques that allow teachers to differentiate the learning process for students with learning disabilities. Chapter 5 describes a series of tutoring techniques that may be employed in the inclusive classroom to assist the teacher in providing differentiated instruction for all the students in the class in a timely fashion. Chapter 6 presents a variety of assessment models that allow for differentiation of evaluation requirements for various students in the class.

Chapter 7 is a more focused chapter that demonstrates the application of many of these strategies in the area of reading instruction for the elementary and middle grades. Because reading disabilities are some of the most common disabilities among students with learning disabilities, I felt that a chapter that specifically addressed reading was essential in this text, and although writing or math disabilities negatively affect some students with learning disabilities, reading is—for most students with learning disabilities—more critical, and no text can address all types of disabilities.

In addition to the focus on differentiated instruction, another subtle yet important theme that runs through the book involves *relationships*. I believe that the most important single factor in the learning process is the relationship between a teacher and a pupil and that this critical relationship—not strategies or instructional tactics—provides the basis for effective instruction. Perhaps because this book focuses on a wide variety of instructional strategies and tactics, I felt a need to make this statement up front—that the basis of effective teaching is a caring relationship. For learning to take place effectively and efficiently, students must be absolutely convinced that the teachers care for them and that the students' learning and, more fundamentally, the students' well-being are at the heart of the teachers' interest. Only from that caring position will teachers be effective in motivating students to involve themselves in their learning. Furthermore, and perhaps in a more basic sense, only from that caring perspective will teachers be motivated to implement the strategies required by the differentiated instruction concept. This relationship theme is apparent in certain sections of the text, such as the self-management section in which a teacher motivates a student to begin attending to his or her own attention and/or learning behaviors. Also, in using scaffolded instruction, the teacher must attend intimately to the student's learning to determine when to withdraw the scaffold or support the student's learning efforts; this instructional decision can be based only on intimate knowledge and understanding of a student's learning technique, and thus a relationship between the teacher and the pupil is critical. Again, the single most important aspect of learning in today's classrooms is the relationship between a pupil and a teacher, and based on a rich relationship, the strategies identified herein will enhance student learning and allow students with learning disabilities to shine!

Finally, I hope that both the special educator and the general educator realize that almost all of these strategies will work as well for

> The most important single factor in the learning process is the relationship between a teacher and a pupil, and this critical relationship—not strategies or instructional tactics—provides the basis for effective instruction.

students with other disabilities, as well as for many of the other lower achieving students in the class. Thus, teachers are encouraged to experiment with differentiated instruction, adapt these strategies to their specific situation, and generally make these work. Again, these strategies and tactics truly represent the "best practices" for students with learning disabilities today.

Differentiated Instruction for Students With Learning Disabilities

Strategies Included in This Chapter:

✔ Differentiated Instruction and Classroom Organization

✔ Cubing

✔ The Bender Classroom Structure Questionnaire

✔ Ten Tactics to Foster Attention Skills

✔ Ten Tactics for Structuring the Lesson

Students with learning disabilities (LD) have a way of challenging almost every general education teacher because of the learning characteristics that are displayed by many kids with learning disabilities. As every veteran teacher realizes, students with learning disabilities may be less engaged in the learning task, unable to cope with multiple instructions, and poorly organized in their thinking and work habits. When these deficits are coupled with fairly severe academic deficits, the result can be a student who is very challenging for general education teachers. In my workshops nationally, I've found that teachers are hungry for tactics and ideas that work for these challenging students.

The concept of *differentiated instruction* is based on the need for general education teachers to differentiate instruction to meet the needs of diverse learners in the general education class; this includes students with learning disabilities as well as a number of other disabilities.

Differentiated instruction may be conceptualized as a teacher's response to the diverse learning needs of a student (Tomlinson, 1999, 2001). Teachers must know the learners in the class, understanding not only such things about each learner as the learning style and learning preferences but also showing a concern for each student by tailoring instruction to meet the needs of each individual student. Given the teacher's professional observations of a student's learning, the teacher would concentrate on modifying (i.e., differentiating) the learning in three areas:

- *Content* (what is learned)
- *Process* (how the content is taught)
- *Product* (how the learning is observed and evaluated)

> The concept of differentiated instruction is based on the need for teachers to differentiate instruction to meet the needs of diverse learners in the general education class.

The learning *content* involves what students are to master, what we want the students to accomplish after instruction (Tomlinson, 1999, pp. 1-65; Tomlinson et al., 2002, p. 46). The content may be delineated in state-approved curricula, in scope and sequence charts (i.e., objectives grouped by subject area and grade level), in state or national standards, or in the curriculum material itself. In most cases, the teacher will not be able to control the specific content that must be covered, but he or she will have control over how to modify that content for presentation to the students based on the learning styles of the students, and in that modification process, some content will be emphasized more than other material (Tomlinson, 1999).

The learning *process* involves how the student interacts with the content, and those learning interactions will in part be determined by the various learning preferences of the students (e.g., is this student an auditory learner, a visual learner, a learner who needs concrete demonstrations, etc.). Because of the diversity of learning styles and preferences demonstrated by students today, the differentiated classroom will typically involve a wide array of activities to address the different learning needs of everyone (Gregory & Chapman, 2002, pp. 9-17; Tomlinson et al., 2002, pp. 46-59). These learning processes may include some of the following:

1. *Activating the learning*—the introductory activities that focus on the material to be learned, relate that material to previously mastered material, let the student know why that material is important, and describe what students should be able to do once they learn.

Different learning needs require differentiated instruction.

2. *Learning activities*—involve the actual instructional activities for the students, such as modeling, rehearsal, choral chanting, movement associated with the content, and/or educational games.

3. *Grouping activities*—both individual and group-oriented learning activities should be planned as a part of the learning process.

Finally, the learning *product* will be of paramount importance because demonstrations of learning allow the teacher to determine the students who have mastered the material and those who may need more time and continued instruction (Tomlinson, 1999, pp. 1-65). Again, the learning styles of the students in the class will help determine what types of products the teacher may wish to accept as demonstrations of learning (Gregory & Chapman, 2002, p. 20). In the differentiated learning classroom, it would not be uncommon for a given unit of instruction to have four or five different types of culminating projects that students may choose in order to demonstrate their knowledge of the topic. Art projects, role-play mini-dramas for groups of students, library or Web-based research, multimedia projects, paper-and-pencil projects, written reports, or oral reports all represent excellent projects that students may complete to demonstrate their knowledge. This assessment component is discussed more completely in Chapter 6.

Using this model of differentiated instruction, the teacher will constantly modify his or her classroom organization, curriculum, instructional methods, and assessment procedures to address the individual learning needs of the students in the class (Gregory & Chapman, 2002, pp. 1-37; Tomlinson, 1999). Furthermore, the teacher's relationship with and knowledge of the students in the class will be the basis for the differentiations in instruction, and so the relationship between the teacher and the pupil is critical. Only a solid positive relationship and fairly complete knowledge of the student's learning styles and preferences can provide an effective basis for differentiated instruction.

As an example of the type of differentiated instructional modification that typifies the differentiated classroom, several authors have suggested the idea of *cubing* (Cowan & Cowan, 1980; Gregory & Chapman, 2002; Tomlinson, 2001). Cubing is a technique that will assist students to consider a concept from six points of view, by giving students suggestions on how to conceptualize a particular concept. While envisioning the six sides of a cube, the student is told that each side represents a different way of looking at the idea (as presented by Gregory & Chapman, 2002, pp. 1-15).

Cube Sides	Function	Use Terms Like
Side one	Describe it	recall, name, locate, list
Side two	Compare it	contrast, example, explain, write
Side three	Associate it	connect, make design
Side four	Analyze it	review, discuss, diagram
Side five	Apply it	propose, suggest, prescribe
Side six	Argue for/against it	debate, formulate, support

Using this idea of cubing, the same concept is looked at from six different perspectives, and the various levels of knowledge of different students may be addressed in this context (e.g., some students consider initial descriptions of the concept, whereas others are involved in analysis of it). In the differentiated classroom, the teacher will intentionally construct his or her lessons based on this cubing concept, and that will emphasize to the students that concepts covered in this fashion are multidimensional and must be considered in a more complex fashion. In studies of President Kennedy's and President Johnson's response to North Vietnam's and China's growing influence in the nation of South Vietnam, the various sides of the cube would suggest that students should do the following:

Describe that response	Buildup of U.S. troops in Vietnam
Compare the response	To French buildup of troops fifteen years earlier
Associate the response	To other presidents' attempts to limit power of other nations in other regions (e.g., President Wilson's response to Germany in 1916)
Analyze the response	Discuss the reasoning of Presidents Kennedy and Johnson
Apply alternatives	Suggest how other presidents chose to limit influence at other times (e.g., the Jefferson administration's response to pirates around the African coast)
Argue the response	Debate the wisdom of Kennedy's and Johnson's response

In using this cubing concept, the lessons will be differentially aimed at one or more aspects of the cube, and students will be exposed to instruction based on a broad array of activities (Gregory & Chapman, 2002, pp. 1-56). Thus, the differentiated classroom is founded on a variety of lesson formats, learning processes, and products that are developed by the students.

In many ways, this entire text is founded on the concept of differentiated instruction and places a priority on the content modifications, instructional differentiation, and setting variations that allow the teacher to meet the needs of students with learning disabilities as well as the other diverse learners in today's classrooms. Although subsequent chapters focus on instructional modifications of content and assessment, this chapter focuses on the setting for differentiated instruction by asking, What type of class structure does a teacher establish? A moment's reflection reveals that how a teacher structures and operates his or her class will initially determine how much differentiation of instruction is possible. Consequently, in this and subsequent chapters, the three components of differentiated instruction noted above will be addressed as a backdrop or foundation for the various teaching strategies described.

TEACHING AS A REFLECTIVE PROCESS

Teaching is at its best a highly reflective process, in which professionals engage in dialogue with themselves and others about strategies that work well and strategies that do not. Such a dialogue can be critical for instruction of students with learning disabilities. Another emphasis throughout this text will be an emphasis on this reflective process.

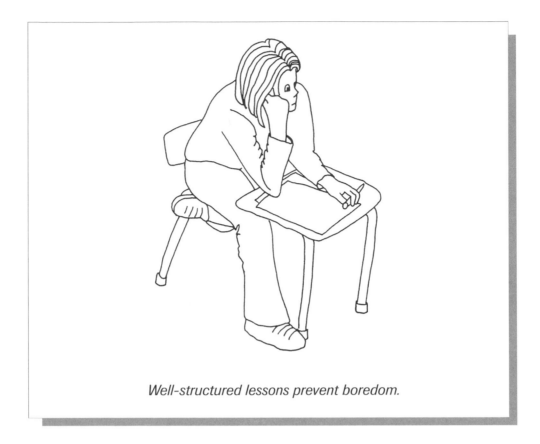

Well-structured lessons prevent boredom.

Teachers will be encouraged to engage in various reflective exercises to focus on the strategies provided and how those strategies may be adapted for various classroom situations. Initially, we will consider the structure of the classroom.

Most beginning general education teachers adopt a structure, organization, and instructional style for their class that is similar to the structure used by their cooperating teacher in their student teaching experience. These teachers arrange their desks in a similar fashion to their cooperating teacher, and many find that they teach in a similar fashion. Of course, this often allows a beginning teacher to implement a class structure that is appropriate and effective because most cooperating teachers are selected because they are believed to be effective teachers. In fact, most beginning teachers do not specifically reflect on their overall classroom organization until one or two years after they begin their career.

However, veteran teachers—teachers with two or more years' successful experience—tend to engage in a reflective process related to structuring their classroom and often improve on their room organization as well as their instructional technique. This reflection can be critical in dealing with students with learning disabilities because both instructional and disciplinary endeavors must begin with intentional structuring of the classroom to maximize effective instruction and minimize disruption. Students with learning disabilities do tend to function much more effectively in a highly structured environment, perhaps because disorganization tends to be one general characteristic of this group of students. Thus, regardless of whether the organizational issue deals with desk arrangement in the class or with the most effective method to study a particular section of the text, highly structured classes and assignments tend to facilitate learning among students with learning disabilities. When contemplating the instruction for students with learning disabilities, a teacher's first emphasis should be a general reflection and reconfiguration of the instructional space and instructional approaches to more easily differentiate the instruction in the class and thus accommodate the needs of students with learning disabilities in the differentiated classroom.

> Veteran teachers—teachers with two or more years' successful experience—tend to engage in a reflective process related to structuring their classroom and often improve on their room organization as well as their instructional technique.

What Is Classroom Structure?

In helping teachers reflect on their classroom structure, the first issue concerns definition; what is classroom structure? Is it merely how desks are arranged, or does it also involve how assignments are structured and delivered, or perhaps how students spend their time? In my work, I have found it more effective to use an expanded definition of classroom structure. Of course, the first level of classroom structure involves how one organizes one's classroom furniture and equipment, and some consideration must be given to placement of desks, arrangement of computers, and so on. However, classroom structure in the differentiated classroom also involves several other levels of structure, such as how a teacher, as the instructional leader, structures the time of the students, as well as how the specific assignments are structured. High levels of organization within specific assignments will tend to result in better performance from students with learning disabilities, and this chapter, as well as several other chapters in this text, will include suggestions for specific structuring of assignments. Teaching Tip 1.1 provides some additional thoughts on the components of classroom structure.

Self-Evaluation of Classroom Structure

Perhaps one way to get an understanding of how one structures one's classroom is to use an informal self-evaluation and look critically at the structural components of the class. Approximately twelve years ago, I saw the need for teachers to reflectively consider their class

---

☞ **Teaching Tip 1.1**

What Is Classroom Structure?

For our purposes in this text, classroom structure means the following:

- The arrangement of furniture
- The establishment of learning centers
- The arrangement of instructional computers and other devices
- The instructional grouping patterns for students
- The orchestration of students' learning time
- The structure of communication between teacher and students, as facilitated or restricted by elements of classroom organization
- The structure of the content of the lessons, the learning processes, and the instructional activities aimed at increasing the variety of learning activities

---

structure and, within that context, a variety of instructional techniques for students with learning disabilities. As a result, I developed the Bender Classroom Structure Questionnaire (BCSQ) (Bender, 1986, 1992; Bender, Smith, & Frank, 1988). The indicators on the BCSQ were specifically selected to represent the types of instructional practices that encourage differentiated instruction and have been shown to facilitate effective inclusion of students with learning disabilities (Bender, 1986, 1992). This questionnaire has now been used in a variety of subsequent research investigations on how both special and general education teachers structure their classroom (Bender & Beckoff, 1989; Bender et al., 1988; Bender & Ukeje, 1989; Bender, Vail, & Scott, 1995). As a first reflective exercise, teachers may wish to use this form and evaluate their classroom structure and differentiated instruction practices. The questionnaire is presented in Teaching Tip 1.2.

📖 **REFLECTIVE EXERCISE: EVALUATION OF MY CLASS**

Using the BCSQ, determine the number of instructional indicators that represent instructional tactics used at least once each week in your class. Consider which techniques you would like to use more frequently, and note some ideas on how you may implement those ideas this week.

☞ Teaching Tip 1.2

The Bender Classroom Structure Questionnaire

Name _____   Date _____

This self-evaluation rating is designed to measure various aspects of instructional environments in order to assist in making useful instructional improvements. It will take about fifteen minutes to complete. Please fill in each blank below, then rate your classroom on each question on the 5-point scale ranging from *only rarely* (i.e., less than once a month) to *almost always* (almost every day).

How many years have you taught school? _____

In what areas are you certified to teach? _____

How many years have you taught students with disabilities? _____

What is your current teaching assignment? _____

How many courses specifically on teaching students with disabilities have you completed? _____

How many students with learning disabilities are in your class currently (during any one period)? _____

How many students total are in that class? _____

		Only Rarely				Almost Always
1.	I keep the lesson moving along quickly	1	2	3	4	5
2.	The class reviews assignments when I return them	1	2	3	4	5
3.	Several students may be walking around in my class at any one time retrieving materials	1	2	3	4	5
4.	Students receive verbal praise from each other	1	2	3	4	5
5.	I encourage students to share various techniques that may help them memorize facts in class	1	2	3	4	5
6.	The class emphasizes correction of worksheets	1	2	3	4	5
7.	Students must raise their hand before standing	1	2	3	4	5
8.	I ask, "How did you learn that?" or some other question to focus on learning strategies	1	2	3	4	5
9.	I insist that doors be shut and students remain in their seats to minimize distractions	1	2	3	4	5
10.	New material is introduced fairly rapidly	1	2	3	4	5

(Continued)

☞ **Teaching Tip 1.2** (Continued)

11.	I suggest particular methods of remembering	1	2	3	4	5
12.	Peer tutoring is used to assist slower learners	1	2	3	4	5
13.	I emphasize the importance of working quietly	1	2	3	4	5
14.	I determine early in the year if a student needs the same concepts covered in different ways	1	2	3	4	5
15.	I use physical touch, such as a pat on the back, as a reinforcer	1	2	3	4	5
16.	I praise students for successful work whenever possible	1	2	3	4	5
17.	Students are encouraged to help each other informally on learning tasks	1	2	3	4	5
18.	I try to determine how students learn best	1	2	3	4	5
19.	I use reading materials that highlight the topic sentence and main idea for slower learners	1	2	3	4	5
20.	I individualize in my class when necessary	1	2	3	4	5
21.	Students are taught to use their own inner language to give themselves silent task instructions	1	2	3	4	5
22.	I use class privileges as rewards for work	1	2	3	4	5
23.	I use a specialized grading system that rewards effort for pupils with disabilities	1	2	3	4	5
24.	I use several test administration options such as oral tests or extended time tests	1	2	3	4	5
25.	Directions for educational tasks are kept simple and are demonstrated to achieve clarity	1	2	3	4	5
26.	Differential curriculum materials are selected based on the learning characteristics of particular students	1	2	3	4	5
27.	I routinely vary the instructional level for different ability children doing the same task	1	2	3	4	5
28.	Instructional materials are varied for different students	1	2	3	4	5
29.	I constantly monitor the on-task behavior of my students	1	2	3	4	5
30.	I individualize my class for low-ability students	1	2	3	4	5
31.	Visual displays and transparencies are used in class to aid comprehension	1	2	3	4	5

(Continued)

👉 Teaching Tip 1.2 (Continued)

32. Students use self-monitoring to record daily
    academic and behavioral progress   1   2   3   4   5

33. A token economy is used for reinforcement   1   2   3   4   5

34. I use the dry-erase board frequently to explain
    concepts   1   2   3   4   5

35. I have an assertive discipline plan in effect   1   2   3   4   5

36. Cooperative learning groups are frequently used   1   2   3   4   5

37. I use individual behavioral contracts with students
    to improve behavior   1   2   3   4   5

38. I use advance organizers to assist students in
    comprehension of difficult concepts   1   2   3   4   5

39. Students complete direct daily measures of
    progress in class   1   2   3   4   5

40. A set of class rules is on display in my class   1   2   3   4   5

Scoring the BCSQ

Scoring the BCSQ may be done either formally or informally. Because these techniques generally represent "best practices," a higher score on the BCSQ is more desirable and indicates that a teacher is employing the instructional techniques that should facilitate successful inclusion. To get a general score, one may merely total the circled score for each indicator, resulting in a score that ranges from 40 (the lowest possible score) to 200.

Bender (1992) reported that a group of 127 general education teachers in Georgia (from Grades 1 through 8) generated a total score of 143 ($SD = 19$) on this questionnaire. A group of 50 teachers from New Jersey (Grades 3 through 12) generated a score of 139 ($SD = 19$) on this scale. These general scores may provide some indication of how you provide varied instruction for students with learning disabilities in your class.

SOURCE: From "The Bender Classroom Structure Questionnaire: A Tool for Placement Decisions and Evaluation of Mainstream Learning Environments" by Bender, W. N. (1992). *Intervention in School and Clinic, 27,* 307-312. © 1992 by PRO-ED, Inc. Used with permission.

Use of this questionnaire will give teachers an initial sense of how well and how frequently they may be implementing various tactics and strategies that have been proven successful for students with learning disabilities in the inclusive general education class. Of course, no one would be expected to implement all of these differentiated instruction practices at any given time or in any one specific period. Still, students will be more successful in classrooms where a variety of these approaches are frequently implemented, and this tool will provide the caring, thoughtful teacher with one mechanism that can foster reflective thought on how one teaches. On the basis of this informal self-evaluation, we may now consider the various components of classroom structure.

INSTRUCTIONAL GROUPING FOR EFFECTIVE INSTRUCTION

In inclusive classes, teachers frequently teach eighteen, twenty-two, or twenty-eight students during each lesson, and to individualize the learning in any form, teachers many years ago began to form instructional groups within the class. Of course, differentiated instruction is based, in part, on effective grouping of students, as has been discussed in the educational literature. There are a variety of options available to general education teachers for structuring instructional groups (Gregory & Chapman, 2002, pp. 57-79). However, many teachers believe that the large numbers of students in the typical inclusive class necessitate whole-group instruction. In fact, this single teaching mode accounts for the largest percentage of the instructional time even in today's classrooms (Elbaum, Moody, Vaughn, Schumm, & Hughes, 2000). However, within the past decade, there has been some debate about the effectiveness of whole-class lecture/discussion as an instructional model, and research has suggested that small-group, teacher-led instruction may be a more effective instructional procedure for students with and without disabilities (Elbaum et al., 2000). Clearly, the general education classrooms should be structured to facilitate, as much as possible, various small-group instructional arrangements.

As an alternative grouping arrangement, research has also supported the use of students to tutor each other (Mortweet, Utley, Walker, Dawson, Delquadri, Reddy, Greenwood, Hamilton, et al., 1999; see also the subsequent chapter on peer tutoring). Even when students with special needs are involved in the tutoring, the research has been generally supportive. This is why a number of indicators on the BCSQ deal with varying the instructional group arrangement rather than always using a whole-group, teacher-led discussion. In fact, the differentiated classroom is characterized by a variety of instructional grouping patterns.

Recently, in many general education classes, the older instructional model of lecture/whole-group discussion seems to be giving way to more appropriate models of instruction that will benefit students with learning disabilities in their academic efforts, and classes that offer a variety of instructional grouping options will tend to be more successful for students with learning disabilities. However, there is still a place for whole-group instruction in the inclusive class. Activities such as morning exercises, simulation games, sharing time, multimedia instruction, class presentations, or social skills instruction seem to be activities that would be most effective as whole-group activities. Furthermore, these whole-group activities would require a space in the class—an area that allows all of the students to attend to the teacher at the same time. Consequently, any class will need to be physically arranged to accommodate a variety of instructional activities, including whole-group activities; teacher-led, small-group instruction; peer tutoring; and individual learning opportunities. These classroom arrangements will facilitate the teacher's ability to differentiate instruction.

> Students will be more successful in classrooms where a variety of instructional approaches are frequently implemented.

REFLECTIVE EXERCISE: HOW DO I TEACH?

1. What percentage of the time in my classroom do students spend listening to me deliver content?

2. What percentage of the time in my classroom are students engaged in group work on projects with their peers?

3. What percentage of the time in my classroom are students engaged in individual inquiry?

4. What percentage of time in my classroom are students engaged in producing products resulting from their learning?

A Recommended Room Arrangement Model

Considerations of room organization for both inclusive general education and special education classes must be guided by concerns about the need to differentiate instruction, the types of activities planned, the number of students in the class, and the behavioral or academic problems demonstrated by those students. Both inclusive general education classes and special education classes, although involving different numbers of desks, may still be arranged based on a few straightforward considerations. Many of these classroom-structuring suggestions have been identified over the years (Hewett, 1967; Wang & Birch, 1984; Wang & Zollers, 1990), and the discussions below reflect these classroom-structuring guidelines.

In an ideal classroom, space would be used to allow for varying instructional tasks at the same time. Although not every classroom has optimum space, Figure 1.1 presents an initial suggestion for arrangement of desks, learning centers, study carrels, computers, and so on in a general education classroom to facilitate differentiated instruction.

This suggested room arrangement includes areas for large- and small-group instruction, as well as individual seatwork, computer-assisted multimedia instruction, and work in study carrels. Perhaps the most notable feature is the semicircular desk arrangement. In this arrangement, students with challenging behaviors should be seated near the teacher, but not together, because they would model inappropriate behaviors for each other! Furthermore, using this arrangement, the teacher can more easily monitor students' behavior visually. Specifically, the teacher can visually monitor each student's work while assisting a particular child; he or she should merely remain outside or behind the semicircle. This arrangement allows the teacher to face almost all members of the class almost all of the time (even when leaning over a student's shoulder to assist on a particular assignment). This ease of visual monitoring will tend to improve behavior and assist students with learning disabilities in the class. A similar semicircular arrangement is also appropriate for special education classes, which generally include smaller numbers of students.

Again, to facilitate differentiated instruction for students with learning disabilities, a teacher must physically arrange his or her classroom to allow for instructional variations, and a variety of instructional areas will be necessary. These typically include various learning centers, a teacher's worktable, and a group work/social skills area. These areas will, of course, vary according to grade level, but differentiated instruction will make higher levels of success for students with learning disabilities more likely. Below are brief descriptions of the various instructional areas that may be appropriate in your class.

Learning Centers

Learning Center Structure. Learning centers should be included to allow for modifications and adaptability of instruction within the classroom context in almost every classroom because the activities and information in the learning center can provide one way to address the diverse needs of a wide variety of learners, including students with learning disabilities (Gregory & Chapman, 2002, pp. 105-110). For the elementary education classroom, learning centers in both reading/language arts and math would seem to be a minimum. Other teachers, depending on

Figure 1.1. General Education Room Diagram

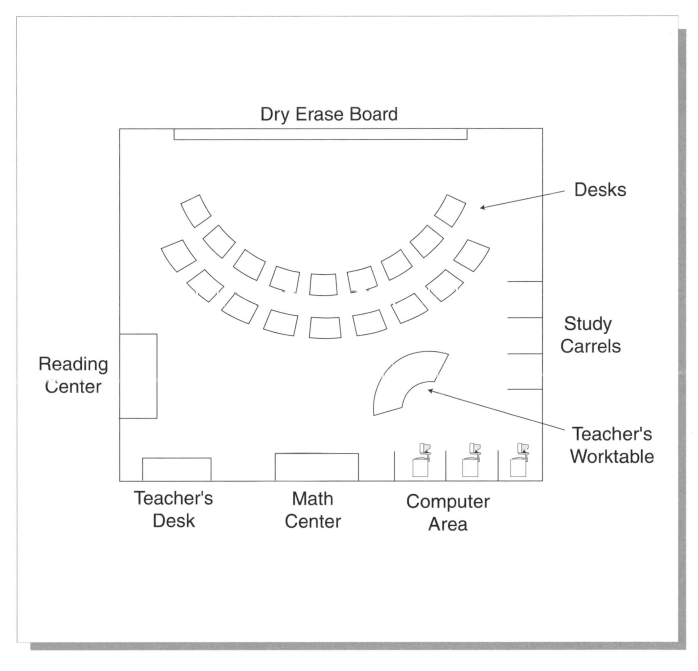

their class grade level and teaching responsibilities, also include a center for science, social science, and/or other subject areas.

For secondary subject area teachers, various centers may be adapted for the subject content. Many history and/or social studies classes, as one example, may include versions of the following learning centers:

Daily Living Center	Government Center
Commerce Center	International Relations
Political Center	Timeline Art Center

As these examples suggest, in content areas (e.g., in this case, history) in departmentalized schools, the learning centers should be based on general concepts or issues within the topic that are not particular to a given unit of study. Thus, in the history centers mentioned above, the teacher would place materials in these centers that were appropriate for the various historical periods and/or different units of study, and although those materials may change when studies of one period conclude and another historical period begin, the learning center names and orientations remain constant throughout the year.

> A semicircular desk arrangement allows the teacher to face almost all members of the class almost all of the time.

Learning Center Materials. The materials that should be included in each learning center should be obtained on a continuous basis and subsequently labeled and organized in a way to facilitate the student's retrieval of appropriate materials. Students with learning disabilities should be taught how to obtain their own work materials from the learning center because this will assist them in the development of organization skills as well as an ability to focus on the specific task at hand. Thus, the learning centers must be a model of efficient organization of materials.

Initially, in establishing a learning center, the teacher should inventory the class and the school's media center to get some idea of the educational materials already available. These may include books, charts or wall posters, bulletin board kits, computer software, educational games, manipulatives, and game boards for multiple uses. Most teachers develop sets of worksheets that may be used, either individually or by small groups of students, and place these worksheets in the learning centers as well. Remember, teachers should seek out the media specialist and inquire whether materials are available for long- or short-term loan to a particular class. In many cases, with special permission, the teacher may be able to check out materials for use for a week, a multiweek instructional unit, or a month. Teachers will also want some materials for lower level readers to use. This will enable almost all students to obtain assignments from the learning center.

In each learning center, teachers should provide some instructions for the students working there. Many teachers post "activity cards" on the wall in each learning center that instruct the students on the activities that must be accomplished to receive credit for completing the work in that center. To make these learning centers accessible for students with learning disabilities, teachers should keep the instructions for these activities simple and clear. Also, classes may have various levels of assignments present on these activity cards and instruct some students to complete the "Level 1" activities while others complete "Level 2" or "Level 3" activities. Again, such differentiated instruction must be provided to meet the needs of students with learning disabilities or other diverse learning needs.

Teacher's Worktable and Desk

The teacher should have a worktable located such that the teacher can scan the entire room while working with one student or a small group of students at a time. This will greatly facilitate the teacher's use of small-group, teacher-led instruction, as the recent literature recommends. Although this requires that the worktable be located somewhere at the front of the room, it does not have to be the focal point within the front area. As long as the teacher has easy visual contact with all members of the class, any location toward the front of the class will do.

I generally recommend that teachers not use the teacher's desk as the worktable. The desk is typically used for writing assignments and grading papers at the end of the day, along with bookkeeping matters, such as lunch money collection and attendance records. Consequently, desks tend to be cluttered with a lot of non-instructional material—some of which may be confidential—and if students are working with a teacher on that desk, the opportunities for misbehavior are multiplied. In contrast, the worktable can be kept clear of everything except the instructional materials in use for the students working there. Also, with a worktable somewhere in front of the class (to ease the teacher's visual monitoring of students), the teacher's desk may be located at any place in the room.

> Students with learning disabilities should be taught how to obtain their own work materials from the learning center because this will assist them in the development of organization skills as well as an ability to focus on the specific task at hand.

Group Instruction Area

Many social activities, such as sharing time, group games, or class projects, require or may best be facilitated by a group instruction area. In inclusive classes, this area may, of necessity, be the student's desk area because twenty-five or thirty desks do tend to fill up a room. However, in some smaller classes, the students may complete group projects on the floor in a nonfurnished, carpeted corner of the classroom. These group

The teacher's desk usually doesn't have room for student group work.

instruction areas generally include some nearby shelves for storage. A screen for viewing films together may also be placed here.

Computer/Multimedia Instruction Area

The use of computers and/or multimedia instruction (e.g., a language master that reads words) has increased rather dramatically in recent years. One would be hard-pressed to find a modern classroom without some multimedia equipment that facilitates learning. In fact, this provides teachers today with a critically important tool for offering differentiated instruction to students with learning disabilities, as well as other learners with special needs. In most general education classrooms, computers will typically be located along the wall, and the electrical outlets may determine where these are placed. In consideration of disciplinary issues for students with learning disabilities, the teacher should make certain that there is ample room between these instructional tools such that distractible and/or aggressive students cannot find too many opportunities for misbehavior. Generally, these should be located in study carrels that are designed for computers and prevent one student from observing another's work.

Study Carrels

Study carrels are essential in classes that include students with learning disabilities because these students may be easily distracted by movement in the class. Generally, several study carrels can be lined up along one wall and may be used for individual seatwork for certain children. In some cases, the students feel better about using these areas if they are labeled an "office." If the class includes a student who is reluctant to work in a study carrel but would benefit from it, the teacher can create a "private office" environment for him or her, merely by labeling a study carrel. One important fact to remember is that if a student with a learning disability needs a place to work that is free of visual distraction, one must be provided to assist the student to remain task oriented.

In addition to limiting the visual distractions that may be present in the work area, teachers should note that many students with learning disabilities are quite disturbed by auditory distraction. Consequently, soft music played continuously in class becomes a type of background noise and may facilitate higher work output from those students. However, one person's relaxation music is another person's distraction. In some instances, teachers may wish to provide soft music through earphones to only one or two students. Regardless, teachers must be careful of the effects of such music on all of the students in the class.

DIFFERENTIATED INSTRUCTION FOR STUDENTS WITH LEARNING DISABILITIES

As indicated previously, this entire text may be considered as a set of ideas for differentiated instruction, and each subsequent chapter presents specific instructional tactics for varying the instruction in the general education classroom. However, in addition to the class-structuring guidelines presented earlier and the ideas in the subsequent chapters, some general teaching tips for differentiating instruction can be offered as initial guidelines for teachers when challenged by students with learning disabilities.

First, the general structure of most classrooms can be greatly enhanced and can be specifically designed to facilitate active engagement by students with learning disabilities by following just a few simple guidelines. Ten tactics for fostering higher levels of attention are presented in Teaching Tip 1.3.

Next, consideration must be given to structuring lessons and developing alternative lessons for students with learning disabilities. Teaching Tip 1.4 presents ten tactics, described originally by Mathes and Bender (1997b), that can guide inclusive teachers in structuring lessons for students with learning disabilities.

☞ Teaching Tip 1.3

Ten Tactics to Foster Attention Skills

1. *Use a highly structured class.* In talking with students and giving instructions in the class, teachers should clearly differentiate between the "floor groupwork area" and the study carrel area. This will help students with learning disabilities understand your vision of the types of work to be done in each area, and higher structure will assist students with learning disabilities in their work overall.

2. *Display classroom rules.* Having a set of three to five positively stated class rules on display can alleviate many behavior problems. Rules that state what a child should do (i.e., quietly complete your work) are usually best, and by referring to the rules when a student is misbehaving, the teacher can, in effect, differentiate himself or herself from the discipline process and make the misbehavior an infraction against the class (i.e., against the rules of the class).

3. *Post a daily class schedule.* Even for teachers in departmentalized schools with forty-five-minute periods, a posted schedule of the day's activities can greatly assist students with learning disabilities in understanding what they should be doing.

4. *Train on class cues.* Teachers should train students to recognize certain cues in the context of the classroom. Depending on the age level, some teachers have a small bell that they ring to get the attention of the class. Others use cue cards that are mounted in front of the class about how to begin a lesson (get out the book, get out your notebook, get out your pencil, etc.). As the cue, the teacher may merely need to point to the chart.

5. *Use two desks.* Hyperactive students frequently get out of their seat without knowing why. For some students, assigning a second desk across the room gives them the ability to move from one to the other periodically (not every five seconds, of course!) without the teaching having to attend to an "out-of-seat" misbehavior.

6. *Use intentional distractions.* For some students with learning disabilities, movement is not only necessary—it is essential. For many of these students, providing them something to do with their hands may alleviate more disruptive movements in the class. This is the concept of "intentional distractions." In short, providing a child with a pen from which he or she can constantly remove and replace the cap provides something to stay busy with during a class discussion (and is usually much quieter than loud pencil tapping on the desk). For pencil tappers, teachers should demonstrate "quiet tapping" (which is tapping on the back of one's own hand). It provides more sensation/stimulation and is quieter than tapping on the desk!

7. *Keep desks clear.* Remind students to keep their desks clear and uncluttered, except for materials and texts used at the moment.

8. *Visually monitor students.* The teacher should arrange the class to allow for visually monitoring the students at all times. Provide verbal reminders to return to task, as needed.

(Continued)

☞ **Teaching Tip 1.3**   (Continued)

9. *Provide color organizers.* Colored organizers can assist many students in organizing their assignments and notebooks. The teacher should work out a color-coded organization system appropriate for the students.

10. *Use peer buddies.* Setting up a peer buddy system in which pairs of students check each other's readiness to begin the next lesson can greatly assist students with learning disabilities in getting through transitions between lessons.

☞ **Teaching Tip 1.4**

Ten Tactics for Structuring the Lesson for Students with Learning Disabilities

Differentiated instruction focuses on the three components of content, process, and product. The tactics presented here offer teachers an array of possibilities to differentiate both the content and the process of instruction.

1. *Provide clear directions.* Providing clear, simple, instructions, particularly during transitions, can assist students with learning disabilities to focus on the learning task.

2. *Provide lesson outline.* A lesson outline will help students focus on what will come next in the small-group or whole-class discussion. From the basis of this outline, the teacher should teach outlining and note-taking skills. This assists students with the learning process.

3. *Develop alternative activities.* To modify the instructional content, when a teacher develops a lesson, he or she should develop a minimum of two worksheets that present the same content at different levels. The use of alternative assignments that cover the same material is one cornerstone of differentiated instruction.

4. *Plan for frequent breaks.* Students who are hyperactive (including many students with learning disabilities) will need frequent opportunities to stand up and move around the classroom. Building thirty-second "stretch-breaks" every fifteen minutes or so into your class period can help alleviate many problems.

5. *Use physical activities.* For all students in public schools, learning is facilitated by movement. Even the learning of the highest achievers in senior high can be enhanced by movement. The emerging research on "brain-compatible education" has documented that the learning process can be greatly enhanced by movement, and if

(Continued)

☞ Teaching Tip 1.4 (Continued)

teachers can tie particular facts to a physical movement and have the class practice that movement, the students with learning disabilities will be much more likely to remember that fact. While some teachers feel that this type of movement-based instruction may be appropriate only in lower grades, a moment's reflection on the popular song/movement combination "YMCA" will indicate that even adults prefer learning associated with movement.

6. *Use clear worksheets.* Teachers should make certain that they do not unintentionally build distractors into the lesson by using cluttered worksheets or instructional materials. For students with learning disabilities who may be visually distracted, such worksheets can result in failure on the assignment.

7. *Decrease task length.* For some students with learning disabilities, a worksheet activity that involves fifty math problems will always appear to be an insurmountable assignment. However, if the teacher prints only fifteen math problems on the worksheet, the student will immediately attempt that assignment. The teacher may then give another worksheet with another fifteen additional problems on it.

8. *Check assignment notebook.* All teachers should require that students write assignments in a notebook, and while many do this, some teachers never check the notebooks. For students with learning disabilities, checking that they have written down the correct assignment can be critical, and the process of checking emphasizes the importance of noting the assignment due dates.

9. *Develop alternative assessments.* Looking at the product of student learning is a critical component of differentiated instruction, and students with learning disabilities, on some occasions, know more about a topic than a paper-and-pencil test can allow them to demonstrate. Teachers must develop and use alternative assessment practices, such as grading open-book homework or class work or using daily databased performance measures. These will be covered in a later section of this text.

10. *Turn to your partner and explain.* The idea behind "turn to your partner and explain this concept" is rooted in the truth that what one can explain, one understands. When conducting a lesson, at various points (perhaps every five minutes or so, when the class finishes a certain amount of material), teachers may have the students pair up and explain those several points to each other, as a comprehension check. Building this routine into the lesson can greatly enhance comprehension of students with learning disabilities.

 REFLECTIVE EXERCISE:
USING DIFFERENTIATED INSTRUCTION

To better understand the overall construct of differentiated instruction, use the list of ten indicators in Teaching Tip 1.4 and identify each instructional modification as either a modification of content, process, or product. Then consider which of these tactics you are currently using in your own class.

What's Next?

With the various options in mind for differentiated instruction, as well as the suggestions above for organization of the classroom, the next chapter will focus more directly on differentiated instruction by varying the instructional process, as dictated by the individual needs of the learner. In particular, a brief synopsis of the information from the brain-compatible literature is presented, along with several strategies that encourage students to take personal responsibility for their learning.

Brain-Compatible Instruction and Personal Responsibility for Learning

Strategies Included in This Chapter:

✔ Ten Tactics for a Brain-Compatible Classroom

✔ Self-Monitoring for Attention Behaviors

✔ Self-Regulation for Class Preparedness

✔ The Responsibility Strategies

Within the past decade, our understanding of how human beings learn—specifically, how the human brain and central nervous system function—has led to an array of recommendations concerning how teachers should instruct students in the public school classroom (Leonard, 2001; Richards, 2001; Sousa, 2001a; Sylwester, 2000). In addition to considering how classes should be structured to differentiate instruction for students with learning disabilities, teachers must also attend to this body of knowledge about teaching practices that are founded on the emerging research on the human brain (Sousa, 1999).

Although a number of instructional practices are rooted in this brain-compatible research (many of these are presented below), one overriding principle is the critical importance of getting students involved with their learning and assuming personal responsibility for their learning. Thus, after a discussion of the recommendations from the brain-compatible instruction literature, this chapter will present several specific strategies that result in students with learning disabilities taking personal responsibility for their academic efforts—self-monitoring, self-instruction, and the responsibility strategy for enhancing behavior in the learning environment.

> One overriding principle is the critical importance of getting students involved with their learning and assuming personal responsibility for their learning.

WHAT IS BRAIN-COMPATIBLE INSTRUCTION?

Brain-compatible instruction (sometimes referred to as brain-based learning) has emerged only within the past decade and is based primarily on improvements in the medical sciences (Leonard, 2001; Sousa, 2001a, pp 1-25). In fact, much of our increasing understanding of the human brain has come from the development of the functional magnetic resonance imaging techniques (a technique that is sometimes represented in the literature as the fMRI). This is a non-radiological technique—and thus a relatively safe brain-scanning technique—that has allowed scientists to study the performance of human brains while the subjects concentrated on different types of learning tasks (Richards, 2001). The fMRI measures the brain's use of oxygen and sugar during the thinking process, and from that information, physicians can determine which brain areas are most active during various types of educational tasks (Sousa, 1999, pp. 1-20). For example, specialists have now identified brain regions that are specifically associated with various learning activities such as language, reading, math, motor learning, music appreciation, or verbally responding to questions in a classroom discussion (Sousa, 2001a).

Many researchers have suggested that the research has developed to a point where specific teaching suggestions may be made. On the basis of this growing understanding of how students learn, teachers across the nation have begun to restructure their classroom practices based on these guidelines (Sousa, 2001a; Sylwester, 2000). Although various authors make different recommendations, the 10 tactics for a brain-compatible instruction classroom, presented in Teaching Tip 2.1, represent the accumulated thought in this area (for additional suggestions, see Gregory & Chapman, 2002; Richards, 2001; Sousa, 2001a; Sylwester, 2000; Tomlinson, 1999).

Teaching Tip 2.1

Ten Tactics for a Brain-Compatible Class

1. Provide a safe, comfortable learning environment.
2. Provide comfortable furniture.
3. Provide water and fruits to students.
4. Structure frequent student responses.
5. Pair physical movement to learning tasks.
6. Use visual stimuli for increasing novelty in the learning task.
7. Use music and rhythms for learning.
8. Provide adequate wait time.
9. Give students choices.
10. Use students to teach each other.

REFLECTIVE EXERCISE: A PREDICTION EXERCISE

Prior to reading the discussion below about the ten brain-compatible instruction tactics, review the list in Teaching Tip 2.1 and make predictions concerning how these tactics may be tied to the emerging brain-compatible research. Read the information below to check your predictions.

A Safe, Comfortable Environment. Research on learning has demonstrated that the brain serves as a filter on several levels. First, the brain selectively focuses on sounds, sights, and other stimuli that threaten our safety, often to the exclusion of other stimuli. A second priority is information resulting in emotional responses, and only as a last priority does the brain process information for new, nonthreatening learning tasks (Sousa, 2001a, p. 43). Thus, based on this filtering or prioritizing brain function, several implications for the classroom come to mind. Clearly, students must not be distracted by a sense of danger in their learning environment; they must feel safe and comfortable in order to be prepared to focus on new material (i.e., the school curriculum) that, by its very nature, is usually not threatening. For students who come from violent homes or communities, who may be picked on at school, or who may frequently feel punished by the school environment, learning new material will be almost impossible. However, physical safety is not enough; for students to feel comfortable, students must feel emotionally secure. Thus, a positive personal relationship with the teacher is paramount. Only in the context of such a comfortable, caring relationship will students with learning disabilities turn their attention to mastering new tasks.

Of course, this holds serious implications for students with learning disabilities because some students may suffer from a sense of frustration in certain classrooms. Students with disabilities may even experience some school classes as "hostile terrain" in which they are frequently punished by either their continuing failure in learning tasks or by the teacher. Clearly, this classroom environment will not support strong academic success for those students.

> The brain selectively focuses on sounds, sights, and other stimuli that threaten our safety, often to the exclusion of other stimuli.

Comfortable Furniture. As a part of structuring a comfortable learning environment, many teachers bring "house furniture" into the classroom and set up readings areas with a sofa and perhaps several comfortable chairs. Lamps are also used in brain-compatible classrooms for more "homelike" lighting, and some research has suggested that lighting closer to the red end of the light spectrum functions like a "wake-up" call for the brain.

A moment's reflection on the hardness of the wooden desks in most of our nation's classrooms—desks in which students must sit in for up to five hours each day—makes this a critical concern for many teachers. How would any adult like to sit in those wooden desks for five or six hours each day for an entire year? A different type of furniture can make our classrooms more user-friendly and facilitate learning.

Water and Fruits. Research has shown that the brain requires certain fuels—oxygen, glucose, and water—to perform at peak efficiency (Sousa, 2001a, p. 20). Up to one-fourth of the blood pumped in our bodies with each heartbeat is headed for the brain and central nervous system, and fluids are critical for even blood flow. Furthermore, water is essential for the movement of neuron signals through the brain (Sousa, 2001a, p. 23). Finally, we now know that fruits are an excellent source of glucose for the brain, and research has shown that eating a moderate amount of fruit can boost performance and accuracy of word memory (Sousa, 2001a, p. 22). Thus, in brain-compatible classrooms, individual water bottles are usually present on the desks for students to take a sip whenever they need to; water is not a once-an-hour privilege in the brain-compatible class. Also, many teachers offer light fruits as snacks.

Frequent Student Responses. Students will learn much more when work output is regularly expected from them because students are generally much more engaged in the process of learning when they must

Brain-compatible classes use comfortable furniture.

produce a product of some type (again the differentiated instructional emphasis on the products of learning!) (Gregory & Chapman, 2002, pp. 37-46). For this reason, students must be required to do assignments, either in the form of class work or homework on any new material that is presented. The frequency of work expected from the students will be a major determinant of how much information students retain. However, the required work output doesn't have to be an entire page of problems—more frequent output of only a few problems each time will be much more useful in the learning process for students with learning disabilities (Sousa, 2001a). More frequent, shorter assignments also give the teacher additional opportunities to check the students' understanding of the concepts covered.

Learning With Bodily Movements. Have you ever wondered why motor skills such as swimming or riding a bike are usually remembered forever, whereas the skills involved in speaking a foreign language are quickly forgotten if not constantly practiced? The emerging research on the human brain has addressed this question concerning motor learning versus higher order cognitive learning, and two findings have emerged. First, learning of motor skills takes place in a different area within the brain—the cerebellum, which is a more fundamental level—than learning of languages. Second, the brain considers motor skills more essential

---

☞ **Teaching Tip 2.2**

Movement-Based Instruction in Higher Grades

Carolyn Chapman (2000) shared a movement-based instructional technique for the upper grades, using movement to illustrate a map of the world. The body parts coupled with the following movements represent the locations of the seven continents and the equator. While facing a map of the world on the wall, students should be taught to do the following movements from memory.

1. Left arm/hand extended, palm open. While left hand is out, reach over with right fist, touch left palm, and say, "This is North America, where we live."

2. Now move right fist to touch forehead and say, "This is Europe."

3. Stick right hand out, palm open, touch that palm with left fist, and say, "This is Asia."

4. Put both hands on hips and say, "This is the equator."

5. Put hands together over one's belt to make a diamond (i.e., left thumb touching right thumb, left fingertips touching right fingertips) and say, "This is Africa. Part of Africa is above the equator and part is below it."

6. Stick left leg out and say, "This is South America."

7. Stick right leg out and say, "This is Australia."

8. Point to the floor between the feet and say, "This is Antarctica; very cold down there."

SOURCE: Adapted from Chapman, 2000.

---

to survival. Because our ancient ancestors often had to run away from predators or, alternatively, had to hunt for their own food, motor movement has been prioritized by the brain as a survival skill (Sousa, 1999). Consequently, motor skills, once learned, are remembered much longer than cognitive skills such as language usage. This suggests that whenever possible, teachers should pair factual memory tasks with physical movements. For example, various spelling works may be taught by moving the arms and legs to the shape of the letters in the word. Even in the upper grades, various memory tasks can be represented by physical movement, and this will greatly enhance retention for students with learning disabilities as well as most other students. An example of this movement technique for learning the location of the continents is presented in Teaching Tip 2.2. This modification involves a change in the process of learning for students who seem to do better with physical movement as a learning support. The contents of other maps can easily be represented with body parts, as can various other learning tasks (e.g., parts of a business letter).

I recently assisted a student teacher in a secondary class to develop a movement technique for demonstrating the living processes at the cellular level in the human body. The lesson required an instructional demonstration that represented a cell involved in the processes of protecting the cell from bacteria while letting in various enzymes. Initially, three big male students stood together facing inward, and locked their elbows tightly to represent the cell wall. We then pointed out that "the cell wall is very strong to protect the cell." Next, we selected a bacteria (i.e., another student) to try to break into the cell, with the cell wall holding that bacteria out. "Cell walls protect the cell from bacteria." Finally, we had a student, representing the friendly enzyme, move toward the cell wall to gain entrance. For our demonstration, we used one of the young women in the class, and the cell wall let that person in without delay. "Cell walls let in food and friendly enzymes." As you can see from these several illustrations, the only limit on the use of this technique in the upper grades would be the limit of the teacher's creativity.

> Because our ancient ancestors often had to run away from predators or, alternatively, had to hunt for their own food, motor movement has been prioritized by the brain as a survival skill.

Learning With Visual Stimuli. Although teachers have known that visual stimuli often enhance learning, this commonsense insight has been confirmed by the brain-compatible instructional literature (Sousa, 1999). Teachers should use color enhancements, size, and shape enhancements in developing lesson materials posted in the classroom because the human brain and central nervous system are specifically attuned to seek out novelty and differences in stimuli (Sousa, 2001a, p. 27). Thus, highlighting the topic sentence of the paragraph in a different color for students with learning disabilities can be of benefit for them in describing the topic of the paragraph. Likewise, using different colors for different parts of speech (red for nouns, blue for verb, green for adjectives, etc.) can facilitate learning. However, to make color an effective learning tool, the teacher and the student (or the class) should specifically discuss why certain aspects of the material are colored differently and the importance of those colored items. Many computer-assisted instructional programs are making use of this technique today and include color highlights to teach syllabication and other reading skills. Again, this represents a modification of the learning processes for students with learning disabilities.

Using Chanting, Rhymes, and Music. Because music and rhythms are processed in a different area of the brain from language, pairing facts to be learned to a musical melody, or a rhythmic chant, can enhance learning. Most adults, on reflection, can remember the song that was frequently used to memorize the ABCs—the tune to *Twinkle, Twinkle Little Star*—and many students used that same song for other memory tasks in the higher grades—the periodic table or division math facts. Again, teachers have used this insight for a number of decades, but the emerging research on the human brain has documented the basis for enhanced learning when music and rhythms are used.

Wait Time. Students have learned that teachers will often call on the first one or two students who raise their hand after the teacher has asked a question in class. Thus, all that students with learning disabilities have to do is remain "invisible" for a few seconds (i.e., not raise their hand and not look toward the teacher), and the teacher will usually call on someone else. On average, teachers will wait only one or two seconds before calling on someone for an answer, and this period of time between the question and when an answer is called for is defined as "wait time" (Sousa, 2001a, p. 128). However, students process information at different rates, and the brain research has demonstrated the importance of waiting for a few seconds (perhaps seven to ten seconds) after asking a question, prior to calling on someone for the answer. This increased wait time gives students who process information more slowly and deliberately a period of time to consider their answer and, it is hoped, raise their hand to volunteer a response to the teacher's question. For this reason, adequate wait time can be a critical component of learning for students with learning disabilities, many of whom do process information more slowly than others in the class.

Student Choices. Sylwester (2000) emphasized the use of choices for students. In short, if teachers want their students to make reasonable and informed choices when they are not in the context of the school, teachers must offer choices and coach students in making informed choices within the context of the classroom. Such choices may involve the options for demonstrating competence or understanding a set of facts, or other choices among assignments on a particular topic.

Using Students to Teach Others. It has often been noted by veteran teachers that having students explain new information to other students can enhance learning, and the emerging research on the human brain has once again supported this instructional procedure. Teachers should get in the habit of presenting some information (the brain research suggests presenting new information at the beginning of the period for between ten and twenty minutes) (Sousa, 2001a, p. 90) and frequently pausing during that presentation and have students reflect on the new information together. The teacher should present information for two to three

All students with learning disabilities have to do is remain "invisible" for a few seconds (i.e., not raise their hand and not look toward the teacher), and the teacher will usually call on someone else.

minutes, get to a stopping point, and then say something such as the following:

Turn to your learning buddy beside you, and take turns explaining the four points I just made. Let me know if you uncover any disagreements in what each of you heard.

The teacher should then move around the room for one to two minutes, listening to the discussions between the students and checking that the students do have a correct understanding of the information just presented. This instructional procedure will result in much higher retention than merely presenting new information in a lecture format because students will have to take personal responsibility for the material, as they explain it to their peers.

THE SELF-MONITORING TACTIC: PERSONAL RESPONSIBILITY FOR LEARNING

Throughout our nation's history teachers have taken the perspective that education is a process done to and for students. Students have been viewed as passive recipients of the educational process, and active participation of students in planning their own learning has not been encouraged. Of course, this view was a serious problem for students with learning disabilities because these students are much more likely to become distracted and uninvolved in the learning process than other students.

In contrast to the view of students as passive recipients of learning, Daniel Hallahan and his coworkers, in their studies of students with learning disabilities, postulated that students must begin to plan a task and assume some personal responsibility for their efforts in attending to a task and learning (Hallahan, Lloyd, & Stoller, 1982; Hallahan & Sapona, 1983; Rooney & Hallahan, 1988). Recent research on the human brain and learning has demonstrated the importance of executive function. *Executive function* is the term that represents the thought processes involved in planning a task, or considering how to undertake a task, rather that specifically doing a task. Prior to actually initiating a task, successful students take a moment to consider what a task requires and how a task may be accomplished; this is executive function. Educators now realize that the success of education is, in large measure, dependent on the responsibility students take for their own learning and behavior (McConnell, 1999), and the brain-compatible instructional literature has supported this view quite dramatically; students must be involved in their learning. Furthermore, students with learning disabilities must be intimately involved in the tasks of learning if learning is to take place. In short, it is very difficult if not impossible to teach anyone anything unless they are willing and motivated to learn. The self-monitoring strategy presented here addresses this requirement for individual responsibility for attending to the educational task.

> Teachers today know that education is an active process and requires student involvement.

The self-monitoring strategy involves teaching a student how to pay attention; attention in the context of the classroom typically means the ability to repeatedly check one's own orientation and focus on a particular task (McConnell, 1999). Whereas early research concentrated on the use of self-monitoring to enhance attention of students with learning disabilities (Hallahan et al., 1982; Hallahan & Sapona, 1983; Rooney & Hallahan, 1988), more recent work has focused on using self-monitoring procedures to enhance classroom readiness behaviors (McConnell, 1999; Snyder & Bambara, 1997) or eliminate behavioral problems that may prevent learning (Shapiro, DuPaul, & Bradley-Klug, 1998). Each of these areas is discussed below.

Self-Monitoring for Attending Behavior

Although teachers through the ages have often told children to "pay attention," very few teachers have ever taught a child exactly *how* to pay attention. The fact is, teachers tend to assume that students know what we mean by that frequently used phrase, "pay attention." However, experience with students with learning disabilities tells us that these students do not stay on task as well as other students; in short, students with learning

> Educators now realize that the success of education is, in large measure, dependent on the responsibility students take for their own learning and behavior.

disabilities do not really know how to pay attention. The attention problems and poor task orientation often noted among students with learning disabilities suggest this deficit in the skill of paying attention among these students. Thus, the initial application of self-monitoring procedures involves teaching students with learning disabilities how to attend to a learning task. This training procedure may be done in either the special education classroom or the inclusive general education classroom by following the steps below.

Identification of the Student. As with all aspects of differentiated instruction, the first task of the teacher is to select the right strategy for the student. Again, this will depend on the teacher's relationship with the students, the teacher's knowledge of the students in the class, and the types of learning problems demonstrated by each student. Hallahan and Lloyd (1987) have suggested several guidelines for identifying the type of students for whom self-monitoring may be an effective intervention. First, the self-monitoring strategy to improve on-task behaviors is intended for students with learning disabilities who demonstrate rather benign attention problems, such as poor task orientation or an inability to complete worksheets on time, rather than overtly aggressive behaviors. This strategy is not effective for children who do not perform their schoolwork because of violent behaviors or noncompliance in the classroom, though variations of self-monitoring procedures have shown some success, even with these severe behavior problems.

Second, self-monitoring should not be used when a student is being introduced to a new topic or learning task. This is not a strategy to be used during the initial instruction phase of learning. Rather, self-monitoring is most effective when a student is in the independent, drill-and-practice phase of learning. Seatwork and paper-and-pencil tasks in any basic skill area are appropriate. Also, self-monitoring is more effective for "speeding up" a student than for increasing the student's accuracy in problem completion (Snider, 1987).

Components of the Self-Monitoring Tactic. During a self-monitoring project, the student is trained to periodically ask himself or herself a very simple question—"Was I paying attention?"—to increase his or her attention skills. The only materials used in this self-monitoring procedure are (1) a "record sheet" on which the student will record his or her attention behavior and (2) a cue to record the behavior—usually a tape recorder with an audiotape of a bell that rings periodically. In making a record sheet, the question above should be printed on the sheet at the top, along with places to answer either "yes" or "no" to the question. This question provides the student with a simple memory technique that tells what should be done (i.e., paying attention to the worksheet and the problems it contains). Whenever the student is cued to consider his or her "attention behavior," the student should silently ask, "Was I paying attention?" He or she should then answer the question on the record sheet and return immediately to work. A record sheet developed by Hallahan et al. (1982) is presented in Teaching Tip 2.3.

> Teachers tend to assume that students know what we mean by that frequently used phrase, "pay attention."

The second component of the tactic is an audiotape that will cue the student to ask the question and mark the record sheet. A cassette tape should be prepared by the teacher that presents a series of bell tones. The time interval between these bell tones should vary from ten to ninety

☞ Teaching Tip 2.3

Self-Monitoring of Attention Record Sheet

Was I Paying Attention?

YES	NO

seconds, but the average time interval should be around forty-five seconds. Teachers can easily make such an audiotape by sitting at a piano and recording a middle "C" (or any single note) at various intervals for approximately twenty minutes. The student will use the tape as the cue to ask the question above, mark an answer, and return to work. For inclusive classes, teachers may wish to have the student use headphones to listen to this bell tone to prevent disruption to other students during seatwork.

> The self-monitoring strategy to improve on-task behaviors is intended for students with learning disabilities who demonstrate rather benign attention problems.

Initial Instruction in Self-Monitoring. Hallahan et al. (1982) also recommended a series of instructional steps by which the teacher actually teaches attention skills. On the first day, the teacher begins instruction by suggesting that the student could finish the work faster and more accurately by learning how to pay attention better. This possibility is discussed with the student in an attempt to have the student accept responsibility for the self-monitoring procedures. The dialogue presented in Teaching Tip 2.4 was recommended by Hallahan et al. for this initial self-monitoring instruction.

📖 REFLECTIVE EXERCISE: REVIEWING THE DIFFERENTIATED INSTRUCTION COMPONENTS

Review the dialogue presented in Teaching Tip 2.4, and consider the three differentiated instructional components (content, process, and product). What specific teaching techniques are presented in this dialogue that represent one of these components of differentiated instruction? For example, the "modeling of attention and inattention" presented here would be one instructional example of modifying the processes used to teach self-monitoring. Can you see other examples of these three processes in this dialogue?

This dialogue presents a discussion of exactly what paying attention means. The teacher should sit in the student's desk and model eye contact with the educational task (worksheet, the reading book, or the blackboard). Also, the teacher may model several off-task behaviors such as staring out the window, playing with a pencil, or talking to other students. The student should then complete a work activity consisting of a set of problems in any subject area while wearing a headset and listening to the bell tone. Each time the student hears the bell, he or she should mark either yes or no on the recording sheet and return to work.

Teaching Tip 2.4

Self-Monitoring Instructions

"Johnny, you know how paying attention to your work has been a problem for you. You've heard teachers tell you, 'Pay attention,' 'Get to work,' 'What are you supposed to be doing?' and things like that. Well, today we're going to start something that will help you help yourself pay attention better. First we need to make sure that you know what paying attention means. This is what I mean by paying attention."(Teacher models immediate and sustained attention to task.) "And this is what I mean by not paying attention." (Teacher models inattentive behaviors such as glancing around and playing with objects.) "Now you tell me if I was paying attention." (Teacher models attentive and inattentive behaviors and requires the student to categorize them.) "Okay, now let me show you what we're going to do. Every once in a while, you'll hear a little sound like this."(Teacher plays a tone on tape.) "And when you hear that sound, quietly ask yourself, 'Was I paying attention?' If you answer 'yes,' put a check in this box. If you answer 'no,' put a check in this box. Then go right back to work. When you hear the sound again, ask the question, answer it, mark your answer, and go back to work. Now, let me show you how it works." (Teacher models entire procedure.) "Now, Johnny, I bet you can do this. Tell me what you're going to do every time you hear a tone. Let's try it. I'll start the tape and you work on these papers." (Teacher observes the student's implementation of the entire procedure, praises its correct use, and gradually withdraws his or her presence.)

SOURCE: Hallahan, Lloyd, and Stoller (1982).

On the first day, the initial instruction in self-monitoring takes about fifteen or twenty minutes. This should be repeated (in a briefer form) for the first several days of self-monitoring. The student should use the self-monitoring procedure every day during the initial stage of instruction. This instruction will require ten to fifteen days. At that point, the teacher will have a number of work activities on which the student had the opportunity to finish the work in class; these successes should be pointed out to the student.

Weaning Procedures. The goal of self-monitoring is the establishment of good attentional skills based on the "habits" of attention, rather than being outwardly dependent on behavior charts and tape-recorded bells. Consequently, Hallahan and his coworkers have stressed weaning procedures by which the initial record sheet and the bell tones are withdrawn, leaving the "habit" of continually monitoring one's own attending behavior (Rooney & Hallahan, 1988).

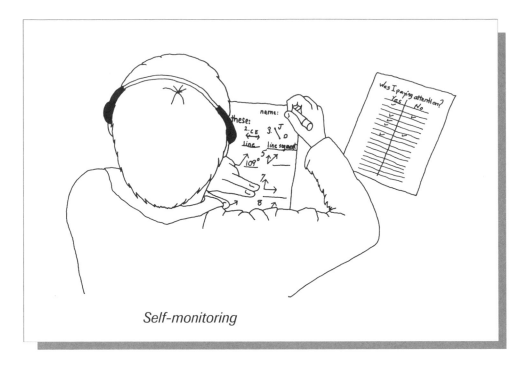

Self-monitoring

Initially, the teacher should wean the student from the bell tones. After a successful intervention period using the full self-monitoring procedure (usually ten to fifteen days), the teacher simply indicates that the student's success in attending to task has increased and that it is no longer necessary to listen to the taped bell sounds. During this weaning phase, the student is encouraged to continue monitoring on-task behavior by asking, "Was I paying attention?" whenever he or she thinks about it. The student should mark the record sheet, and if the student was paying attention, he or she should self-praise (e.g., give yourself a pat on the back!) and then return to the worksheet.

During the next weaning phase, the student is weaned from the recording sheet. The student is given instructions to ask the question whenever the thought occurs and to praise himself or herself for being on task and then to return quickly to the task. Generally five or six days are recommended for each phase of the weaning process (Hallahan et al., 1982).

Efficacy Research on Self-Monitoring of Attention

The research on self-monitoring has demonstrated that this procedure works for students across the grade levels in both special education and general education classes (Rooney, Hallahan, & Lloyd, 1984), making this an excellent strategy for the differentiated classroom in almost any school setting. Next, this procedure may be taught to students in

Teaching Tip 2.5

Using Self-Monitoring

Hallahan, Lloyd, Kosiewicz, Kauffman, and Graves (1979) conducted one of the classic early studies in the self-monitoring research. A 7-year-old boy with a learning disability was used in a single-subject reversal design. The A phases were baseline phases in which both on-task behavior and academic productivity were measured. The B phases were self-monitoring treatments in which both the cue to self-monitor (i.e., a taped bell tone) and a record sheet were used. During the first weaning phase, the cue to record (bell tone tape) was withdrawn, and the child was instructed to record his behavior whenever he thought of it. During the second weaning phase, the recording sheet was withdrawn and the child was instructed to praise himself whenever he was on task.

To measure on-task behavior, several observers were trained to observe the child in class. Also, academic productivity in math and handwriting was measured by counting the number of problems completed by the child on the worksheets that the child turned in. The results demonstrated that both on-task behavior and academic productivity improved during both of the treatment phases. The on-task behavior remained at relatively high levels during the weaning phases in which the tape and the recording sheet were withdrawn. This suggested that the child had internalized the habit of attention (i.e., checking his on-task behavior regularly) by the end of the project.

groups (Hallahan, Marshall, & Lloyd, 1981). Finally, research has shown that almost every student with a learning disability can improve his or her attention using this procedure (Digangi, Magg, & Rutherford, 1991; Hallahan & Lloyd, 1987; Snider, 1987). The on-task behavior of some students has more than doubled (from 35 to more than 90 percent), which is roughly like doubling the educational time in any given year for children with learning disabilities! An early study that demonstrated this level of efficacy is presented in Teaching Tip 2.5.

Research has now addressed a number of additional questions about the use of self-monitoring. First, for students with attention problems severe enough to warrant medication, this self-monitoring procedure can dramatically enhance attention skills above the effects of medication alone (Mathes & Bender, 1997a). Thus, even for students on medication for attention problems, self-monitoring procedures should be used. Of course, this holds serious implications for instruction in almost every general education classroom today. Specifically, how can any teacher justify not implementing a self-monitoring procedure for students on medication for attention problems when we have solid evidence that this procedure will help?

To emphasize the importance of this tactic for students with learning disabilities, allow me to share a personal example that demonstrated how critical this technique can be. As a relatively new higher education faculty member, I taught this self-monitoring technique in a methods class for special education teachers at Concord College, in Athens, West Virginia. In that class, I had an older woman, who was the mother of a fourteen-year-old daughter who had recently been diagnosed with learning disabilities. After assigning some readings on this self-monitoring idea, the mother chose to try it with her daughter while the young girl completed her homework. The mother later shared with me that this seventh-grade girl would sometimes do homework for up to three hours per night and still not accomplish a great deal! Of course, with self-monitoring implemented, that student began to complete her homework in about ninety minutes each weekday evening, and both the mother and daughter were ecstatic, but that's not the end of the story!

> Research has shown that almost every student with a learning disability can improve his or her attention using this procedure.

Within just a few weeks, the daughter had requested that her teacher also allow her do self-monitoring on her school tasks in class (that's when I heard about this little experiment!). The teacher knew me and called to ask what self-monitoring was. Imagine a student with a learning disability asking to try a particular learning method and the teacher not knowing anything about it! Needless to say, I provided some readings and actually met with that teacher to assist her in getting up to speed on this self-monitoring procedure. Still, the importance of this technique in that young girl's life is obvious! She wanted to learn how to use a method that would help her stay on task and save time on her class work and homework.

> For students with attention problems severe enough to warrant medication, this self-monitoring procedure can dramatically enhance attention skills above the effects of medication alone.

This is the only time in my career that I've had this particular experience, and I will never forget how critically important this technique was for one young girl with a learning disability. To state again, I believe that every teacher in general and special education classes should be using some version of this technique for students with learning disabilities. Given the attention problems these students demonstrate, I can think of no technique that is more critical.

Self-Instruction for Increasing Appropriate Behaviors

With the research continually demonstrating the success of self-monitoring procedures for increasing attention among students with learning disabilities, researchers began to apply this self-monitoring concept to behaviors other than attention. In fact, a number of researchers have recently applied the self-monitoring principles to increasing the class preparedness of students with learning disabilities or even decreasing inappropriate behavior (McConnell, 1999; Snyder & Bambara, 1997). For example, McConnell (1999) presented a classroom self-monitoring scale that enabled students to evaluate a number of their classroom behaviors. This check sheet, presented in Teaching Tip 2.6, may be easily modified to fit the exact needs of students with learning disabilities in almost any class, and some form of self-monitoring along these lines will instill in students their responsibility for learning and for being prepared.

> Imagine a student with a learning disability asking to try a particular learning method and the teacher not knowing anything about it!

THE RESPONSIBILITY STRATEGY

What Is the Responsibility Strategy?

The "responsibility strategy" or, more appropriately, the "responsibility strategies" focus on a student's responsibilities in the classroom, as well as on the relationships to the student's teachers, classmates, and school (Bender, 2002, pp. 35-50). Whereas the self-monitoring approach described above places the responsibility for paying attention and class readiness behaviors on the student's shoulders, this strategy offers the opportunity for a teacher to elicit cooperation from students with learning disabilities by offering them serious responsibilities for the successful daily functioning of the class. This can often increase the personal responsibility that students with learning disabilities take for their learning, as well as create smoothly running classrooms.

Some students with learning disabilities derive a certain amount of attention and/or personal power from inappropriate behavior or even oppositional/defiant behavior. During the misbehavior, the attention of the class is centered on the student, and the teacher must attend in some fashion to the misbehavior. This is a powerful position for a student to be in, and some students with learning disabilities (as well as other

---

👉 **Teaching Tip 2.6**

Classroom Self-Monitoring Scale

Name _____   Class _____

Date _____   Teacher _____

Circle one of the four choices: 4 = *always*, 3 = *most of the time*, 2 = *some of the time*, 1 = *did not do.*

1.	Worked without disturbing others	4	3	2	1
2.	Participated in class	4	3	2	1
3.	Listened and paid attention when the teacher was talking	4	3	2	1
4.	Asked for help when I needed it	4	3	2	1
5.	Followed teacher directions	4	3	2	1
6.	Completed class assignments	4	3	2	1
7.	Turned in completed assignments	4	3	2	1

Student Score _____

28-24 points:	SUPER!	19-14 points:	Fair
23-20 points:	Good	13-0 points:	Make a plan!

SOURCE: From McConnell, M. E. (1999). Self-monitoring, cueing, recording, and managing: Teaching students to manage their own behavior. *Teaching Exceptional Children, 32* © 1999 by The Council for Exceptional Children. Reprinted with permission.

---

students) enjoy this type of attention. Indeed, some may find that most of their recognition in class comes from situations in which they *misbehave.*

One effective strategy to use with these kids is based on finding creative ways for offering attention to students who need to demonstrate their personal power in order to fill their need for attention (Bender, 2002, pp. 35-50). Using these students for an individual responsibility allows the student an opportunity to "show off" in an appropriate way, as well as take some direct responsibility for some aspect of the class. I

☞ **Teaching Tip 2.7**

An Illustration of the Responsibility Strategy

Dr. Bob Brooks, a former principal of a lock-door school unit in a psychiatric hospital for difficult kids, often tells of a student—we'll call him Terrance—who broke every lightbulb he could get to within the school. All lights were fair game, and Terrance really didn't care what disciplinary measures were used to punish him for breaking lightbulbs—he was going to break them anyway. This was, quite blatantly, an oppositional and attention-getting misbehavior on the part of the student.

To Dr. Brooks's credit, he reflected on Terrance's relationship to the class and the school in general, and then he took a chance; Dr. Brooks made Terrance the "Lightbulb Monitor" for the school. Each day, Terrance was encouraged to roam the halls for a brief period, visit each room, and ensure that each and every lightbulb was working properly. When lights were out, he had the responsibility of reporting the problem to the office. Of course, Terrance loved going into a room of his peers each morning—filled with his own importance—and switching on the lights several times while the teacher checked attendance. His peers saw that Terrance was given special privileges, along with his special responsibility, and that attention from his peers made a positive difference in his behavior. This responsibility strategy ended Terrance's lightbulb breaking, but perhaps the more important point is that Terrance had a responsibility—a meaningful contribution to make to the school—for perhaps the first time in his school career.

have used the terms *responsibility strategy* or *responsibility strategies* to highlight the critical factor in this instructional tactic—the need to give kids with learning disabilities some meaningful responsibility that they wish to take and that allows them to receive attention for positive behaviors. Furthermore, such behaviors modify the student's relationship to the teacher and/or others in the classroom, putting those relationships on a more positive basis. If students with learning disabilities who are misbehaving can find ways to demonstrate their personal authority and power in productive ways, they will not need to demonstrate that power in disruptive ways. An anecdotal example, presented in Teaching Tip 2.7, can help illustrate this strategy.

A Research-Based Responsibility Tactic

A research-based example of a responsibility tactic comes from Dr. Charles Maher (1982, 1984) of Rutgers University. Dr. Maher reported several research studies in which adolescents with horrible behavior records were used as tutors for students with mental disabilities in lower grade levels. Although the tutors in these studies demonstrated conduct-disordered behaviors rather than learning disabilities, this research does suggest how very effective this tactic can be, even for students with serious behavior problems.

On initial reflection, Dr. Maher's application of this tactic seems frightening for many experienced educators. Imagine finding the "last-chance" students—that is, adolescent males and females in the middle and junior high years who had been identified as socially maladjusted and emotionally disturbed because of violence, aggression, and/or other severe behavioral problems—and using them as tutors! In a very real sense, there was the potential that these adolescents in middle and junior high would actually victimize the students from Grades 2 and 3 whom they were tutoring.

> If students with learning disabilities who are misbehaving can find ways to demonstrate their personal authority and power in productive ways, they will not need to demonstrate that power in disruptive ways.

In fact, the opposite occurred! In the controlled study in 1982, socially maladjusted students with conduct problems who were used as tutors improved their behavior *drastically*, compared to another group of similar students who merely received peer counseling. The number of disciplinary problems for the tutors went down, their attendance improved, and their tutoring even assisted them academically. Furthermore, anecdotal observations suggest that the responsibility of tutoring seemed to be the deciding factor. By virtue of tutoring, these students were seen as "leaders" in some sense, and this was a novel experience for many of these students with behavior problems. Specifically, these adolescents began to "own" their tutees—to "protect" them on the playground and to play with them. In the face of these surprising findings, Dr. Maher repeated this experimental study in 1984, just to ensure that the first results were valid. The results of the second project were the same. Tutoring gave students with behavior problems a serious responsibility for others—a meaningful connection to others in the school—and that responsibility drastically improved their behavior.

When extrapolated to students with learning disabilities, one may well imagine the power of this strategy in improving behavior and

*Responsibility for living things
is the ultimate responsibility.*

setting a positive tone for learning. How often, in the past, have students with learning disabilities received attention for not completing their work on time or for being incorrect in their answers? This strategy can not only increase the responsibility that these students feel for the classroom and the school, but it also offers an opportunity for receiving praise and positive attention for students with learning disabilities for positive work (Bender, 2002, p. 38).

Of course, as in the example above, the limited academic skills of many students with learning disabilities will limit the application of this strategy. Most students with learning disabilities would not be appropriate tutors for students at the same grade level because of the limited academic skills of these students (one exception to this general guideline is classwide peer tutoring, described in a later chapter). However, using students with learning disabilities as tutors of younger children in simpler reading or language arts tasks should work quite well. Again, in the example above, the adolescents were invited to contribute something— they were given a responsibility that they thought important. For the teacher who wishes to implement a differentiated instruction classroom, having this behavioral intervention option is critically important.

REFLECTIVE EXERCISE: YOUR DISCIPLINARY CHALLENGE

Consider your most challenging student, and think of the most recent two or three times you needed to discipline him or her. Have you invited this student to take a meaningful leadership role or responsibility in the class? Is there some responsibility that this student would undertake for the class, which would give this student bragging rights? Is a responsibility strategy right for this student?

Who Should I Use This Strategy With?

> How often, in the past, have students with learning disabilities received attention for not completing their work on time or for being incorrect in their answers?

Students with learning disabilities are often good candidates for using the responsibility tactic because these students will often demonstrate specific strengths on which a responsibility may be founded. For example, given a student with a learning disability in reading and a relative strength in math, the teacher may be able to use that student as a tutor to help weaker students in math or as a "class writer" on the dry-erase board for the math problems each day. Teachers should select the responsibility based on the strengths of the student.

Furthermore, this strategy fits the need in a number of situations in which students with learning disabilities are angry, aggressive, or even oppositional. When a student's need for attention becomes apparent, the teacher should talk with the student about how he or she can "assist" in the class, using his or her leadership skills. The teacher may then suggest something, such as a chore in the classroom, that the student is interested in doing and that gives the student "bragging rights" in front of the other class members.

In using this strategy for students with learning disabilities, one must carefully select a task or responsibility that can be successfully completed by the student in question. These responsibilities should not "challenge" the student; teachers should not use tutoring in academic tasks that tax the tutor academically. Rather, select a task within the student's comfort level, and allow the student an opportunity to succeed and thus to receive positive attention for his or her successful contribution to the class.

Creativity in a responsibility strategy.

Implementing the Responsibility Tactic

When a student with a learning disability has consistently demonstrated a need for attention, the teacher should reflect on the student's opportunity for positive attention in the class, as well as the student's relationship with the teacher and others in the school. It is often effective for the teacher to mentally take several steps back and ask, *"How have I invited this student to positively contribute to this class today?"*

The statement above is phrased quite deliberately: Note the use of the phrase *"How have I invited."* Has the student been *invited* to demonstrate his or her capabilities, leadership skills, and opportunities to present a positive self to the school class? In some cases, the answer is probably that the student with the learning disability hasn't been effectively invited to make an appropriate and meaningful contribution to the class. Educators must deal with large numbers of students almost all of the time, and this may prevent any teacher—even the most effective and sensitive teachers—from giving all the attention required by some students. For this reason, a wise educator will try to find ways to involve every student with a learning disability—to make him or her feel special—by inviting the child to contribute in some appropriate fashion.

Why Give a Behavior Problem Student Responsibility?

Most of us remember dusting the erasers, cleaning the blackboard for teachers, or doing other "teacher's helper" jobs as privileges in the classrooms of our youth. With a moment's reflection, we can remember how special—how important and involved—those relatively boring and mundane tasks made us feel. Of course, students with learning disabilities often do not get to do these jobs because teachers frequently use these jobs as privileges or rewards, and students with learning disabilities do not earn rewards in the general education classroom as frequently as students without disabilities. In fact, when presenting this strategy around the country, I have realized that many teachers feel it may be inappropriate to "reward" misbehavior by using students with poor attention skills or behavior problems for special tasks or responsibilities. Indeed, rewarding misbehavior with a serious responsibility does seem to go against all of our behavioral training (in behavioral thought, one removes a privilege for misbehavior!). Nevertheless, for some students with learning disabilities, offering an attention-generating responsibility will be just the ticket to turn negative behavior into positive behavior and to increase the sense of responsibility the student has for the class. Furthermore, by the time a teacher considers using the responsibility strategy for a student with learning disabilities, the teacher has probably already tried everything else in the intervention tool box and has nothing to lose by trying this strategy!

> A wise educator will try to find ways to involve every student with a learning disability—to make him or her feel special—by *inviting* the child to contribute in some appropriate fashion.

Critical Aspects of the Responsibility Tasks

In seeking an appropriate task, the teacher should consider the interests and desires of the student with the learning disability, his or her capabilities, and the needs of the classroom. The possible task options are almost endless. This is why I frequently refer to this strategy in the plural—that is, responsibility *strategies*. The task that a student is assigned is relatively unimportant, and almost any necessary task (or even some unnecessary ones—e.g., lightbulb monitor) will do. However, at least two things are important.

1. The student must feel that he or she is truly given an opportunity to contribute (i.e., he or she must have impressive "bragging rights" for the opportunity to do the task).

2. He or she must feel that the task is important. The student must be made to feel like a contributing partner in a task that he or she values (Bender, 2002).

How can a teacher find the "right" responsibility for a student with a learning disability? Often the students' actions will tell you. For example, the student described earlier was fixated on lightbulbs, and the role of lightbulb monitor was perfectly appropriate for him. The teacher should try to consider a student's hobbies and interests, as well as the needs of the class or school. Does the school need pictures taken? Could the school use someone to report gang graffiti on playground walls? Could adjudicated students with learning disabilities (appropriately supervised by teachers, of course) take some responsibility for notifying teachers about verbal fights on the playground? If planned appropriately, any of these tasks could represent an effective contribution to the school and a positive responsibility.

> Students with learning disabilities need to earn rewards in the general education classroom as frequently as students without disabilities.

Of course, in selecting the responsibility, teachers should consider issues such as students' confidentially, privacy, safety, and legal liability. For example, don't appoint a "bathroom" monitor (unless you want a student peeking into bathroom stalls!). Furthermore, no student's responsibility should require that he or she leave campus or get involved in physical altercations that have already begun between other students. The principal, because of required training in school law and so forth, is an excellent contact to make when considering responsibilities that involve students with learning disabilities. Also, supervision should always be available for any student completing his or her responsibility.

In addition to routine supervision, remember that students may need to be more closely supervised the first few times they try out their responsibility. In implementing tutoring as described in the example above, you should consider how and what type of training to offer tutors. How much supervision will be necessary for those tutors, and what types of reinforcement can be offered them? For example, do they get to leave the classroom a few minutes early to go to tutoring? Leaving the classroom takes place in front of the peers and indicates a great deal of trust, thus providing a great deal of reinforcement for students with learning disabilities. However, leaving the classroom also places the student in an unsupervised hallway.

> Supervision should always be available for any student completing his or her responsibility.

Using the Responsibility Tactic

With these general suggestions and concerns in mind, the responsibility strategy can focus a student on his or her contribution to the class and to the school at large while emphasizing his or her importance as well as responsibility to the class. Students with learning disabilities often "bloom" when offered the opportunity for positive attention because their previous schooling may not have included many opportunities for attention. Thus, teachers should employ this strategy whenever possible and be as creative as necessary by actively seeking ways to involve students in their academic learning.

CONCLUSION

This chapter has presented several guidelines from the brain-compatible instruction literature, and these relatively new instructional techniques will greatly enhance the academic options for students with learning disabilities in the classroom. Although not all of these tactics are applied in every class all the time, the achievement for the students with learning disabilities in the inclusive class will improve with increasing implementation of these teaching ideas.

Foremost in the brain-compatible instructional literature is the emphasis on helping a student become involved in and responsible for his or her own learning. The self-monitoring strategy and the responsibility strategy described above will assist the student in gaining some control over his or her attention behaviors and off-task behaviors in the general education class, and when a student with learning disabilities senses increasing self-control over these behavior problems, there are usually positive results in self-esteem as well. Thus, the most important strategies for teachers to use involve helping the student gain control over his or her behavior problems.

What's Next?

The first two chapters of this text have presented strategies for differentiating instruction in terms of room organization and emotional support/personal responsibility of the students; the next chapter presents two complementary models for structuring the academic instruction for students with learning disabilities.

Differentiating the Learning Process

Scaffolded Instruction and Metacognition

Strategies Included in This Chapter:

✔ Guidelines for Effective Scaffolding

✔ A Scaffolding Example: The Story Map

✔ Metacognitive Instruction

✔ Advance Organizers

✔ Graphic Organizers and Study Guides

✔ Reconstructive Elaborations

✔ Questions Associated with Pictures in Text

✔ Reciprocal Teaching

THE NEED FOR STUDENT SUPPORT

Students with learning disabilities and many other learners in the classroom demonstrate a variety of academic deficits as well as deficits in planning and various other organizational problems, and, of course, the concept of differentiated instruction places strong emphasis on the diverse learning needs of the students (Tomlinson, 1999, pp. 1-60). Whereas appropriate classroom structure and organized assignments will support students with learning disabilities in their personal organization of schoolwork, these students will also need highly organized academic instruction and numerous academic supports for understanding the tasks assigned to them. Thus, in addition to the supportive physical and emotional environments described in Chapters 1 and 2, students with learning disabilities need various supports to master academic material, and this chapter focuses on two approaches that provide such academic support: *metacognitive instruction* and *scaffolded instruction.* Although the theories behind these approaches developed somewhat independently, each of these approaches supports the overall emphasis of differentiating instruction based on the needs of the learner (Tomlinson, 1999), and many would argue that these approaches are quite similar. After a brief overview of these two instructional paradigms, this chapter will focus on several specific metacognitive and scaffolded instruction techniques that will assist teachers in differentiating the instructional processes, based on the needs of the diverse learners in each class.

Why Metacognition?

Metacognitive instruction has developed over the past two decades and is one of the most influential concepts in the field of learning disabilities today. The growing emphasis on metacognition is quite understandable, given the characteristics of the students we teach. Every veteran teacher has experienced the "dog ate my homework" story from some student with a learning disability. Indeed, most of us have contemplated asking, "Why did you put your homework on the floor, where the dog could reach it?" In reality, students with learning disabilities often do the homework and then leave it on the desk or a bed where "Rover" can get to it; they may also put the paper on the desk at home, on the sofa, or even on the floor—presumably as "dog munchies." The point is they often do the work but don't put that work in their bookbags to get it to school the next day. Still, that makes little difference in the long run because they frequently forget to bring their bookbags to school anyway! In short, even when students with learning disabilities perform the required work, there is no assurance that their relative deficit in organizational skills will allow them to present that work to the teacher.

With these deficits in organization noted, teachers may easily understand why students with learning disabilities have so much difficulty with schoolwork. For example, consider a fifth-grade class in which the teacher makes the following assignment.

> *OK, class. Since our social studies assignment involves writing our congressperson, I want you to put up your social studies books. Take out your language arts texts, and turn to page 189. On that page you will find the format for a business letter, and I want you to write a sample business letter to your congressperson, using that form. Billy will write the address for you on the chalkboard.*

This assignment involves a minimum of four different instructions—which must be followed in sequence in order to ensure success—as well as several additional critical pieces of information (including one piece of information that is not even available yet—the address on the board!). Given the organizational problems noted above, why would teachers expect students with learning disabilities to successfully transition into this new task?

> Even when students with learning disabilities perform the required work, there is no assurance that their relative deficit in organizational skills will allow them to present that work to the teacher.

In fact, much of the frustration that teachers feel in dealing with students with learning disabilities stems from failure to successfully transition from one activity to another, and students are often left in the dark because of the complexity of instructions offered for the transition period.

Metacognitive instruction involves providing students with the tools to assist them in improving their organization skills and completing their assignments. The term *metacognition* may loosely be defined as "thinking about one's thinking." This may include a number of different components such as the following:

1. planning the steps necessary to complete a task,

2. ordering those steps into the correct sequence, and

3. monitoring one's progress on those steps.

In short, metacognitive instruction involves providing a structuring mechanism or support for a child to assist in completing the task—it helps students think about their assignment, plan the sequence of steps required, and monitor how they are doing on each step.

In various metacognitive instructional approaches, students are trained to give themselves silent instructions using inner language for task completion while they are doing the task. Because the use of "inner language" or "silent language" is the basis of metacognition, teachers may wish to look over the original self-instructional steps to foster inner language (presented in Teaching Tip 3.1). These were first described by Meichenbaum and Goodman (1969, 1988), and understanding these steps will help in understanding the use of inner language and the concept of metacognition.

Based on research over the past several decades that is strongly supportive of metacognitive instruction, teachers today should incorporate a wide variety of these metacognitive ideas into their teaching (Ashton, 1999; Day & Elksnin, 1994; Gregory & Chapman, 2002, p. 20; Mastropieri & Scruggs, 1998; McTighe, 1990). Furthermore, with consistent and regular practice in these techniques, students will begin to develop their own metacognitive understandings; thus, these metacognitive skills will generalize across classes. Over time, students with learning disabilities will

Kids enjoy metacognitive strategies.

be much better able to plan, organize, and complete complex assignments if they are trained repeatedly using metacognitive instruction (McTighe, 1990).

In fact, many argue that, at a time when knowledge is expanding so drastically, the major focus of education should be not mastery of factual knowledge but mastery of the processes that enable a child to process factual knowledge. In this view, the highest goal of education would be to enable every student to develop into a successful metacognitive thinker—one who carefully considers the various aspects of the available knowledge and its relationship to the assigned task and who then completes the required steps in sequence, monitoring his or her own performance. If this is a realistic goal for educating students with learning disabilities—I would argue that it is the only worthy goal—then a metacognitive instructional emphasis should be readily apparent in every classroom. A variety of metacognitive tactics are presented below.

Scaffolded Instruction

The concept of scaffolded instruction developed more recently than metacognition—over the past fifteen years or so—and was based, in part, on metacognitive understandings. Scaffolded instruction may best be understood as a sequence of prompted content, materials, and teacher

Teaching Tip 3.1

"Silent Language" for Self-Instruction

Imagine a teacher teaching a child with a learning disability in math how to complete a double-digit addition with regrouping problem. Specifically, imagine the several steps in that problem that must be completed in sequence to correctly solve the problem (add the digits in the 1s place. Put the first digit of that answer below the 1s column, and regroup the second digit to the top of the 10s place. . . .). Instructing this student in the "silent language" task instructions represents one early form of metacognitive instruction. Here are the steps.

$$
\begin{array}{r}
35 \\
+27 \\
\hline
62
\end{array}
$$

1. The teacher completes a problem, reciting the independent step-by-step instructions for problem completion. This modeling step encourages the child to respond similarly in later steps.

2. The teacher and student complete the next problem while the student repeats the steps out loud.

3. The student completes the next problem and uses overt self-instruction by repeating the steps out loud. The student should gain confidence with the teacher immediately available to help.

4. The student completes the next problem relatively independently while whispering the step-by-step instructions softly. This is intended to approximate the last step of using "silent language" self-instruction.

5. The student completes the next problem using silent language to provide self-instructions.

SOURCE: Adapted from Meichenbaum and Goodman (1969, 1988).

or peer support to facilitate learning (Dickson, Chard, & Simmons, 1993; Englert, Berry, & Dunsmore, 2001; Larkin, 2001; Stone, 1998). The emphasis is placed on the adult assisting the student in the learning process with individual prompting and guidance, which is tailored to the specific needs of the individual student to offer just enough support (i.e., a scaffold) for the student in a new task. The student is initially considered an apprentice in the learning effort; thus, too little support leaves the student stranded and unable to comprehend the assigned work and complete the task, whereas too much support would prohibit the student from independently mastering the task. Therefore, the level of support must be specifically tailored to the student's ever-changing

> ### ☞ Teaching Tip 3.2
>
> ### Key Features of Scaffolding
>
> While there is no specific "model" for scaffolded instruction, a focus on the major emphases presented by Stone (1998) will assist in understanding the concept of scaffolding.
>
> 1. The recruitment by an adult of a child's involvement and interest in a meaningful and culturally desirable activity that is beyond the child's current understanding
>
> 2. The provision of adult support for the child's learning, based on constant observation and diagnosis of the child's understanding or skill level, together with careful calibration of the support provided to help the child accomplish the goal
>
> 3. The provision, by the adult, of a range of various types of support, including nonverbal assistance, modeling, pointing, and verbal assistance based on various questioning techniques
>
> 4. The assumption that the adult support for learning will be temporary and gradually withdrawn to foster transfer of responsibility of the task from the adult to the child

understanding of the problem. Also, that support would gradually be withdrawn, allowing the student to eventually "own" the task performance. Stone (1998) provided four key features of scaffolding that sum up this process. These are presented in Teaching Tip 3.2.

Although a critical component of scaffolding is the sensitivity of the adult who is supporting the student in the learning process, a variety of structured learning supports may be considered "scaffolds" on which a student may depend in the learning process. Various charts and/or graphics that assist in the learning process would be scaffolds that the student, with adult supervision initially, could use to master newly presented subject matter. One common example would be that of a *story map*.

As noted throughout this text, many students with learning disabilities have difficulties organizing their thoughts during learning tasks, and this is equally true in their efforts to comprehend content material or stories. These students do not understand that, in many reading passages, there is an underlying structure, and as a result they miss the opportunity to use the story structure to enhance their comprehension of the reading passage. For this reason, a number of researchers have encouraged specific instruction in story structure for students with learning disabilities (Swanson & De La Paz, 1998), and such instruction provides a scaffold on which students may explore new stories. Specifically, most stories will include the following:

> information on the story setting and information on several primary characters,
>
> an initiating event or problem for one of the main characters,
>
> a sequence of actions to solve the problem,
>
> a climax describing when and how the main character successfully deals with the problem, and
>
> a conclusion or resolution of the problem.

These rather predictable components may be formulated into a story map that will assist the student with a learning disability to organize his or her thoughts. Thus, when a student with a learning disability reads a story silently in the general education classroom, he or she should simultaneously complete a story map, as a scaffold on which to build understanding of that story. A sample story map is presented in Teaching Tip 3.3.

> Scaffolded instruction may best be understood as a sequence of prompted content, materials, and teacher or peer support to facilitate learning.

This story map activity is also very effective when completed as a "buddy" activity, and two or three students may partner together to complete the map. Furthermore, these story maps should be reviewed in class as a postreading activity to check for accuracy and for comprehension of the reading material. The story map can subsequently be used as a study guide for any future tests on that content. In fact, a wide variety of instructional activities can be built around the story map concept. Thus, teachers in inclusive classes can greatly enhance the likelihood of reading success for students with learning disabilities by simply using a story map as a scaffold for virtually every reading assignment in the differentiated classroom.

Although reading in subject content areas does not usually involve the same components as a story narrative, teachers may use this concept of a story map as a scaffold to assist students with learning disabilities while they are also reading in content areas by developing maps that are more appropriate to the specific content area. Additional examples of instructional scaffolds are presented in subsequent chapters; for example, the discussion of semantic webs in Chapter 7 represents another idea of an instructional scaffold that will assist the teacher in modifying the learning process for learners with various needs in the class.

In translating the scaffolding metaphor into instructional practice, Larkin (2001) provided a set of guidelines and instructional examples for each. These will help the novice understand the scaffolding concept.

👉 **Teaching Tip 3.3**

A Scaffolding Example: The Story Map

Name _____   Date _____

Story Title _____

The story setting was _____

The main character was _____

_____

Other characters were _____

_____

The problem began when _____

_____

_____

Then several important things happened: _____

_____

After that _____

_____

Next _____

_____

The problem was solved by _____

_____

The story ends when _____

_____

It's hard to anticipate where misunderstanding will arise.

REFLECTIVE EXERCISE: COMPARE AND CONTRAST METACOGNITION AND SCAFFOLDED INSTRUCTION

Reflect for a moment on the similarities and differences between scaffolded instruction and metacognitive instruction. Is every metacognitive technique a "scaffold" for the learner? How do these techniques assist the learner with the process of learning?

ADVANCE ORGANIZERS

Origins of the Advance Organizer

An *advance organizer* is a metacognitive technique that enables a student to comprehend the basic organization of the material to be learned prior to actually studying the material. An advance organizer may be defined as material presented "in advance of and at a higher level of generality, inclusiveness, and abstraction than the learning task itself" (Ausubel & Robinson, 1969). The presentation of this type of material allows the student to mentally organize his or her studies of the material to be learned and represents one way to "hook" or "ground" new

☞ Teaching Tip 3.4

Guidelines for Effective Scaffolding

- *Identify what students know.* Effective scaffolding requires that teachers are cognizant of what a student already knows (background or prior knowledge) and of the student's misconceptions (i.e., which competencies are developing and which are beyond the student's current level of functioning) (Pressley, Hogan, Wharton-McDonald, Mistretta, & Ettneberger, 1996). For example, Anna was aware that some of her students "think in terms of money." When she taught "rounding" to those students, Anna used the familiar concept of money.

- *Begin with what students can do.* Laura (not her real name), another special education teacher, was aware of individual student ability levels. When Laura began reading lessons, she gave the students with learning disabilities an opportunity to read something that could be read independently or with little teacher assistance. This enabled students to begin the reading lesson successfully.

- *Help students achieve success quickly.* Laura found that writing and penmanship tasks were laborious for some of her students with written expression disabilities. When she assisted her special education students in the general education classroom for a lesson on storytelling, Laura asked the students to dictate their ideas while she wrote them on paper. This accommodation enabled the students who had difficulty with written expression to generate ideas without worrying how to convey them on paper. Also, Laura served as an adult listener to reinforce the notion that storytelling and written expression are acts of communication and shared experience.

- *Help students to "be" like everyone else.* Miller and Fritz (1998) interviewed a successful adult with learning disabilities about his school history and found that a major theme was the individual's desire to be regarded like other students. These researchers suggested that as much as possible, teachers orient classroom tasks for students' work to be perceived as being like that of their peers. For example, Anna suggested that Mark (not his real name), a struggling student, be moved into a third-grade text like that of his peers. She informed Mark of his responsibility to work hard but also let him know that she would be there to give him the assistance he needed. Anna noted that when Mark was placed in the third-grade math book with her assistance, he was still struggling with math but holding his own. She was confident that she made the right decision to place him in a more difficult math book, with assistance, because Mark felt good about using the same book as his third-grade peers.

(Continued)

Teaching Tip 3.4 (Continued)

- *Know when it's time to stop.* Anna learned from experience that continued drill and practice may not always be effective. She stated, "Overkill erases." Anna found that once her students had demonstrated mastery of a skill, continued practice may result in the students refusing to work or students producing work with numerous errors. For example, when some of Anna's students with learning disabilities were asked to complete a general education math assignment with fifty problems, she noticed that the students completed the first three rows of problems without an error. Students began making numerous errors on the final three rows. Anna found that employing systematic review and purposeful practice with a limited number of math problems was effective. She also noted that just a few written or spoken questions regarding reading or language arts assignments provided needed review without overkill.

- *Help students be independent when they have command of the activity.* Effective scaffolding means that teachers need to listen and watch for clues from their students as to when teacher assistance is or is not needed. Obviously, teachers do not want students to fail, but they should not allow students to become too dependent on the teacher. As special education teacher Beverly (not her real name) noted, achieving independence is different for individual students. Some students may be at identical skill levels, but emotionally they may be at different levels regarding the amount of frustration they can tolerate. Students may not be able to be "weaned" from teacher assistance at the same time. In other words, some students will need more teacher support while learning to perform a task; others will demonstrate task mastery more quickly. Like the mother bird that helps her chicks leave the nest to become independent birds, teachers need to help their students gradually move from teacher assistance to student independence as students demonstrate command of the task or activity.

SOURCE: From "Providing Support for Student Independence Through Scaffolded Instruction." by Larkin, M. J. (2001). *Teaching Exceptional Children, 34*(1), 30-35. © 2001 by The Council for Exceptional Children. Reprinted with permission.

knowledge into existing knowledge. The advance organizer was one of the predecessors to the full development of metacognitive instruction, and much of the subsequent work on metacognition was based on the concept of advance organizers.

One example of an advance organizer was provided by Darch and Carnine (1986) and involved the use of a chart that represented some of the ideas to be described in a science instructional unit on how altitude affects climate and vegetation. A visual display was presented in which a

Figure 3.1. Mountain Advanced Organizer

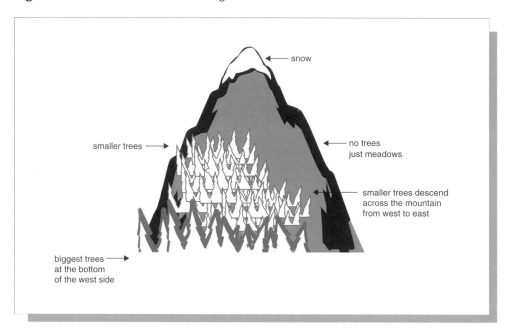

mountain was divided into different shaded areas, which may have looked something like Figure 3.1. Within each shaded area, a description of the types of vegetation for that area was written. At the bottom, the description stated, "Bigger trees at the bottom of the west side." The shaded area above was labeled "Smaller trees." The area above that was described as "No trees, just meadows." The top of the mountain was labeled "Snow." Discussion of this type of chart prior to beginning the science unit can greatly enhance the learning of students; in fact, the chart should remain before the class for the entire unit and would therefore represent a "hook" on which to hang subsequent concepts and understandings.

Research has indicated that advance organizers represent one metacognitive tactic that will improve the content learning of students with learning disabilities across the age span (Darch & Carnine, 1986; Darch & Gersten, 1986; Lenz, Alley, & Schumaker, 1987; Lovitt & Horton, 1994). Teaching Tip 3.5 presents a research study that provided evidence on the effectiveness of advance organizers.

Based on this research, advance organizers should be provided for group projects, interactive lessons, lectures, homework assignments, class work assignments, and other content area instructional activities in almost every activity in the general education and the special education classroom. When class content in general education classes is structured around a set of advance organizers, students with learning disabilities are much more likely to succeed. Furthermore, for inclusive classes, the special education teacher may develop the advance organizer, which can then be used for all students in the class (Bender, 1985).

☞ Teaching Tip 3.5

Research on Advance Organizers

Darch and Carnine (1986) demonstrated the effectiveness of using advance organizers during content instruction in the middle school grades. Twenty-four students with learning disabilities in Grades 4, 5, and 6 were randomly assigned to either an experimental group or a control group. A statistical comparison of these two groups demonstrated no difference in IQ and reading achievement between the groups of students prior to treatment. The control group was taught using traditional text and teacher-initiated group discussion. The experimental group was taught the same science content, by the same teacher, using advance organizers in the form of the visual display of the mountain's climate and vegetation described previously. During the first day of unit instruction, the teacher of the experimental group would show a visual display of the various concepts to be learned. The experimental group received this type of visual display on the first day of each three-day unit of instruction. The students were instructed in this content for fifty minutes on each of nine days. After the nine days of instruction, the students were assessed on both achievement and attitude. Results indicated that the group taught using the advance organizers outperformed the control group on each of several achievement probe tests given during the unit instruction. Also, one of the attitude questions demonstrated that the group using the advance organizers believed that they learned more than the control group. There was no difference on the students' overall enjoyment of the instruction between the experimental and the control group. However, these results do demonstrate that advance organizers can result in higher achievement and possibly a better attitude toward learning.

Graphic Organizers and Study Guides

Graphic organizers and study guides represent adapted advance organizers that can focus students with learning disabilities on the task at hand both prior to and during the task. Study guides and graphic organizers differ only slightly from advance organizers in that the work on a study guide is to be completed during the study of the material rather than prior to it. Study guides may also be referred to as "participatory organizers," with the emphasis on students' participation in completing the study guide during the study itself (Bender, 1985; Dye, 2000).

Lovitt, Rudsit, Jenkins, Pious, and Benedetti (1985) provided the example of a study guide for a secondary science lesson, presented in Teaching Tip 3.6. Students were taught some science content using traditional instruction and subsequently using study guides. The results indicated that provision of a study guide for junior high school science students with learning disabilities resulted in greater gains in achievement than did traditional instruction because the students had to become involved in the lesson in order to complete the study guide. The positive results of using a study guide were demonstrated for high-achieving, normally achieving, and low-achieving students, as well as for students with learning disabilities in the experimental classes. Clearly, provision of study guides facilitates increases in achievement for all students, particularly for students with learning disabilities, and these metacognitive supports should characterize the differentiated classroom at all grade levels.

> Research has indicated that advance organizers represent one metacognitive tactic that will improve the content learning of students with learning disabilities across the age span.

One tactic for general education teachers involves development of a study guide and then using that guide as both an advance organizer and subsequently as a participatory organizer. For example, in using the mountain chart described earlier as an advance organizer, the teacher would show the chart to the students prior to beginning the unit and then ask questions about what the different shaded areas meant. In using the same chart as a participatory organizer, the teacher would reproduce the chart on a worksheet with the shaded areas unlabeled, and the students would be expected to add descriptions to those areas until their worksheets included much more information than the original visual display.

Research has demonstrated the effectiveness of using study guides for students with learning disabilities (Lovitt & Horton, 1994; Lovitt et al., 1985), as well as for other students in the class. Of course, this last point cannot be overemphasized. All students benefit from the use of study guides—not merely students with learning disabilities—which makes this instructional strategy an effective differential instructional strategy for inclusive general education classrooms. Thus, teachers should never view preparation of study guides as additional work that benefits only students with learning disabilities in the class. Rather, in either inclusive classes with coteachers working together or in the single-teacher general education class, study guides will enhance learning for all students.

Although many study guides are based on words and reading skill, as is the previous example, study guides may also be based on charts or pictures to complete or label. Research by Bergerud, Lovitt, and Horton (1988) indicated that study guides in the form of visual displays may work better for some students with learning disabilities than reading-based study guides. Given the wide array of learning styles

☞ **Teaching Tip 3.6**

A Sample Study Guide

Name: _____   Date _____

Learning About Molecules Framed Outline

A. Molecules

1. _____ is made up of _____.

2. A piece of _____ is an _____ when all the
    _____ arc _____.

3. A _____ _____ is made up of _____
    atoms of the same kind.

4. The molecules for _____ is O_2. This _____
    is made up of _____ oxygen _____.
    It is _____.

5. The word *kinetic* means _____.

6. There is a _____ that all _____
    are always _____. It is called the kinetic _____.

7. Many years ago Robert Brown discovered the _____
    _____. He observed _____ grains _____
    in a _____ pattern over surface of _____.

8. Some examples of molecules moving are _____.

> One tactic for general education teachers involves development of a study guide and then using that guide as both an advance organizer and subsequently as a participatory organizer.

demonstrated by students with learning disabilities, teachers should employ an array of study guides emphasizing both pictorial study guides, as well as language/reading-based study guides. Again, the differentiated instructional imperative would suggest that a variety of study guides should be used to vary the learning processes for all learners.

RECONSTRUCTIVE ELABORATIONS

Mastropieri and Scruggs (1988) recommended a mnemonic strategy for content instruction that involves elaborations on the central theme to facilitate recall. Reconstructive elaborations provide more concrete information in a meaningful fashion than do the typical types of examples in text. For example, a typical history text concerning World War I may report that many soldiers died in trenches because of disease rather than combat. However, the typical pictures in those texts would show soldiers in trenches but not the living conditions in those trenches. Mastropieri and Scruggs (1998) recommended using a picture cue that shows soldiers dying in the trenches and falling among the rats that lived in the trenches because such a reconstructive elaboration is more accurate as a teaching tool and aids the memory of students with learning disabilities. A description of a reconstructive elaboration is presented in Teaching Tip 3.7.

Pictures can be a critical tool in aiding memory. In fact, a moment's reflection on Washington crossing the Delaware River during the American Revolution illustrates the power of pictures in aiding memory.

> All students benefit from the use of study guides—not merely students with learning disabilities—which makes this instructional strategy an effective differential instructional strategy for inclusive general education classrooms.

Almost all Americans remember that famous story from the Revolutionary War, when Washington stood in the front of the boat to cross the river in the dead of night and lead his army in the surprise Christmas attack on the winter camp of the British in Trenton, New Jersey. Of course, historians have often pointed out two errors in that picture. First, Washington was probably not standing, exposed to blowing snow and frigid temperatures on that fateful evening; second (and somewhat more certain), the American flag on the back of the boat that was portrayed in that famous picture had not been created at the time of the battle—it was to come several years later. Still, the potency of this image is one component of most Americans'

☞ **Teaching Tip 3.7**

Reconstructive Elaboration on Dwight D. Eisenhower

Facts to be taught. Dwight D. Eisenhower was a general in the United States Army who later became the president of the United States. He was the supreme allied commander during the final years of World War II and planned the famous "D-Day" invasion, in which the allied armies invaded France in order to force the German and Italian forces to leave France and return to their own countries. His election to president was, in large measure, because of his successful leadership in World War II.

Reconstructive elaboration. (Show overhead of Eisenhower represented as the "tower" of a man—that is, taller than others in the picture—with the letters "I Tower" and "WWII" on his breast.) To remember that Dwight Eisenhower was a great general in World War II, remember the words *I-Tower.* That should help students remember his name. See it sounds like Eisenhower to say "I-Tower." What does the "I" mean on his chest? What picture will we think of when we think of Eisenhower? (Elicit responses.) What does the "WWII" on his chest mean? (Elicit responses.) Now close your eyes, and describe this picture to me. Who is the tallest man, or the "Tower," in this picture? (Elicit responses.) What letters are on his chest?

---

understanding of the desperate nature of that cunning surprise attack, and that picture—errors and all—does indicate the power of imagery in learning. Thus, the use of pictures, as memory aids, is one tactic that will assist students with learning disabilities because memories associated with pictures seem to last much longer.

There are several additional issues in the use of reconstructive elaborations for students with learning disabilities. First, development of the reconstructive elaboration pictures can take some time, and although pictures are numerous in almost every textbook, most current textbooks do not include reconstructive elaborations among the pictures presented. Consequently, teachers may have to spend some time developing them. In inclusive classes, this time concern is somewhat abated because the teacher pairs can allow some flexible time for one teacher or the other to develop these reconstructive elaborations and the charts or transparencies that go with them. In single-teacher general education classes, teachers may wish to use students to develop these reconstructive elaborations (what a wonderful assessment of student knowledge this would make—see discussion of authentic assessment in Chapter 6).

In fact, a moment's reflection on Washington crossing the Delaware River during the American Revolution illustrates the power of pictures in aiding memory.

Of course, once such academic supports are developed for use one year, the same reconstructive elaborations can be employed in subsequent years during the same unit. Furthermore, teachers will find that this approach to modification of content appears more frequently in textbooks published in subsequent years because the use of the reconstructive elaborations does facilitate content learning for students with learning disabilities.

REFLECTIVE EXERCISE: STUDENTS' DEVELOPMENT OF RECONSTRUCTIVE ELABORATIONS

Consider the use of reconstructive elaborations that have been developed by members of the class. How could a teacher structure a group activity that would result in development of several reconstructive elaborations by various groups of students? What types of guidelines should be provided to the groups as a starting point (teachers may wish to jot down a few of their ideas about these guidelines)? How can the students gauge the importance of the information that they intend to include in the elaboration? What types of reinforcement could be offered for the most effective reconstructive elaboration?

The very potency of an image or picture presented in text may represent yet another learning problem for students with learning disabilities. Given the previously noted distractibility of students with learning disabilities, some researchers have raised the possibility that too many pictures or other visual cues may decrease learning for these students (Rose & Robinson, 1984). However, other researchers have shown that pictures can greatly improve recall for students with learning disabilities (Mastropieri & Peters, 1987). To address this disagreement in research, we must consider both the *quality* and the *use* of pictures as memory aids in teaching. First, the quality of the pictorial aids involves both the accuracy of the information conveyed in the picture, as well as the importance of that information. Although textbooks, reading books, and most other reading material intended for school use include some illustrations, the quality and use of the illustrations vary widely. For example, there have been examples in the past where the "little red wagon" described in the young child's reading story was colored green in the picture accompanying the story! Clearly, the art department at the publishing house did not communicate with the reading instruction

Teaching Tip 3.8

Questions for Discussion on Important Pictures in Text

1. Why is this picture important enough to discuss in class? What do you see pictured here that may represent a major concept of this unit of instruction?

2. How does this picture fit into the sequence of events discussed in this unit? Should this picture be discussed early in the unit or later? Why?

3. What details in this picture represent important aspects of the unit? How are those details illustrated by this picture?

4. What important things are not pictured here that could have been illustrated? How could those concepts have been incorporated into this picture? Who would like to draw a picture showing those additional facts?

department, and such errors can be quite confusing to young readers, particularly if the plot of the story is dependent on the wagon being red.

Next, the use of the pictorial aids will determine in large measure their effectiveness in helping students with learning disabilities remember important facts. As in the case of the reconstructive elaboration presented above, teachers should talk about various pictures in text, asking questions about why the content in the picture is presented in a particular fashion or how additional content would add to the picture in the text. When teachers use the pictures presented in text as a learning tool—as a subject for class discussion—then the use of pictorial information can greatly assist students with learning disabilities in mastering important content. Teaching Tip 3.8 above presents a series of questions that teachers may use in discussing pictures in texts. In fact, such a discussion of several of the most important pictures in the textbook chapter (the teacher should determine which pictures present enough critical information so as to be worthy of discussion time in class) can be an excellent instructional exercise early in an instructional unit.

The Reciprocal Teaching Technique

Reciprocal teaching represents a scaffolded instructional technique in which the teacher and the content presentation are each providing support for student learning. Eventually, the students become responsible for self-questioning through structured dialogue (Lederer, 2000; Palincsar & Brown, 1986, 1987). The reciprocal teaching method focuses on the things the teacher can do to facilitate the students' planning of the task and task completion. In reciprocal teaching, students are supported by the teacher initially and use four specific techniques to explore a reading passage:

- Prediction
- Question generation
- Summarizing
- Clarifying

The teacher first models these procedures in questions for the group, and subsequently each member of the group becomes the "teacher" and leads the discussions using these same four procedures. Teaching Tip 3.9 presents a sample reciprocal teaching dialogue (Palincsar & Brown, 1986).

A teaching dialogue such as this is exciting for anyone who has ever attempted to involve students with learning disabilities in discussions because many students with learning disabilities are quite reluctant to answer questions in class for fear of potential embarrassment. Not only are numerous students participating in the dialogue below, but the level of this small-group instructional dialogue indicates a great deal of metacognitive understanding on the part of the students. Each of the students in this dialogue was aware of the four basic procedures that are included in reciprocal teaching, and even when the students could not complete one of the goals, they were still aware of the need to complete that particular step (e.g., thinking about what came next in the story). Reciprocal teaching is a scaffold for learning a variety of content and can easily be incorporated into almost any general education classroom. This procedure will greatly benefit students with learning disabilities, as well as many other learners in the class.

> Involving students with learning disabilities in a reciprocal teaching dialogue assures that every child will be involved in using the four metacognitive processes..

Implementation of Reciprocal Teaching

In reciprocal teaching, the teacher and the students take turns as instructional leader. Whoever is the "teacher" assumes the role of leading a dialogue about the reading passage. In the example below, the task is a reading passage that the students must read silently. Using the reciprocal teaching approach, the common goals of each member of the group are predicting, question generating, summarizing, and clarifying. Each of these goals is taught separately.

☞ Teaching Tip 3.9

A Sample Reciprocal Teaching Dialogue

Student 1:	My question is, What does the aquanaut see when he goes under water?
Student 2:	A watch.
Student 3:	Flippers.
Student 4:	A belt.
Student 1:	Those are all good answers.
Teacher:	Nice job! I have a question too. Why does the aquanaut wear a belt? What is so special about it?
Student 3:	It's a heavy belt and keeps him from floating up to the top again.
Teacher:	Good for you.
Student 1:	For my summary now: This paragraph was about what aquanauts need to take when they go under the water.
Student 5:	And also why they need those things.
Student 3:	I think we need to clarify the word "gear."
Student 6:	That's the special things they need.
Teacher:	Another word for *gear* in the story might be *equipment,* the equipment that makes it easier for the aquanauts to do their job.
Student 1:	I don't think I have a prediction to make.
Teacher:	Well, in the story, they tell us that there are many strange and wonderful creatures that aquanauts see as they do their work. My prediction is that they'll describe some of these creatures. What are some of the strange creatures you already know about that live in the ocean?
Student 6:	Octopuses.
Student 3:	Whales.
Student 5:	Sharks.
Teacher:	Listen and find out. Who will be our next teacher?

First, the teacher discusses the benefits of *prediction* as a reading strategy. Prediction of what comes next in the text involves relevant background knowledge of the text and provides students with a reason to read further, that is, to confirm or refute their predictions. Therefore, this strategy involves both comprehension of material being read and comprehension monitoring of material that has already been read. The teacher may even prepare a poster or wall chart of the various aspects of prediction and keep it in front of the class to assist the student who is leading the activity on any particular day.

The second phase of reciprocal teaching is *question generation.* Question generation gives the student the opportunity to identify the type of information that may make up test questions. Also, this activity may provide an occasion to discuss the methods of study for various types of questions.

Summarizing is the third aspect of reciprocal teaching. This step provides an opportunity to integrate information from different sections of the text. The most important ideas of the reading sections should be jointly identified and discussed.

Finally, the fourth activity—*clarifying*—encourages students to identify the major points of the reading selection and to identify concepts that may be difficult. Identification of difficult concepts is one aspect of reading comprehension that is particularly troublesome for students with learning disabilities because these students will often read a selection and not realize that they did not understand part of the passage. Seeking clarification also allows the student to ask questions without embarrassment because the role of the student is to "question and clarify" the problem areas for other students.

> Reciprocal teaching is a scaffold for learning a variety of content and can easily be incorporated into almost any general education classroom.

Each of the four components of reciprocal teaching is taught for a single instructional period, with the teacher conducting these lessons. Initially, each strategy is explained and examples are given along with guided practice. By the fifth or sixth day, the teacher and students are using the strategies together to discuss reading material. At that point, the teacher continues to model the strategies, praises the students for using the strategies, and prompts the students to use additional strategies. Note here the "scaffolded" nature of this student support—the idea that the teacher is constantly modeling, demonstrating, and only selectively turning these responsibilities over to the students as the students' skills increase. By the end of a two-week period, the role of "teacher" is rotated and the students become the facilitators.

Teaching Tip 3.10

Reciprocal Teaching Efficacy

The study by Lederer (2000) illustrated the efficacy of reciprocal teaching for students with learning disabilities in a secondary social studies class. Lederer used six inclusive classrooms, two each in Grades 4, 5, and 6, in a comparison of the effectiveness of reciprocal teaching. The students in experimental classes were taught their social studies for a thirty-day period using reciprocal teaching, while the students in the other classes were taught in the traditional manner. Fifteen students with learning disabilities were in the experimental classes and formed the experimental group, while ten students with learning disabilities were in the control classes and formed the control group. The three dependent measures were measures of the students' ability to answer comprehension questions, generate questions, and summarize, based on a reading selection in social studies. The repeated assessments throughout the thirty-day period indicated a consistent advantage in each dependent measure for the students who received reciprocal teaching instruction. The students with learning disabilities in the reciprocal instruction group consistently outperformed the students with learning disabilities in the control group on question generation, comprehension, and summarizing the reading passages.

Research on Reciprocal Teaching

Several studies have indicated that reciprocal teaching is useful in helping students understand written text (Brown & Palincsar, 1982; Lederer, 2000; Palincsar & Brown, 1986, 1987). These studies used students with various disabilities and concentrated on reading comprehension in the basic skills areas; in each case, reciprocal teaching was demonstrated to be an effective scaffolding technique resulting in improved comprehension of the reading text. One example of a recent research study is presented in Teaching Tip 3.10 above.

CONCLUSION

These tactics represent an array of metacognitive and scaffolded instruction techniques that should be used for students with learning disabilities, as well as other students in the differentiated classroom. While implementing a differentiated instructional approach, teachers often find that these scaffolding and metacognitive techniques provide the basis for an entirely new way of teaching. Metacognitive and scaffolded learning approaches focus the teacher on presenting information in a manner that directly supports the students' academic endeavors. With these supports in place, students with learning disabilities will, in general, perform quite well in inclusive classes. Thus, the responsibility of every general education teacher is clear—we must support the learning of students with learning disabilities using an array of these metacognitive and scaffolded instruction tactics.

What's Next?

In this chapter, a number of metacognitive and scaffolded instructional techniques have been described that will allow the teacher to differentiate the instruction in the classroom based on the needs of the individual students. These techniques are increasingly incorporated into the texts and curriculum materials available for instruction in today's classroom, but the critical aspect of differentiated instruction is the teacher's judgment concerning how frequently to use these techniques and when to withdraw support for a particular student during the learning process. In addition to these general instructional techniques, a series of learning strategies for use in particular types of educational tasks have been developed that are also based on metacognitive theory. These learning strategies are presented in the next chapter, and teachers should note the similarity between strategic instruction and the metacognitive techniques presented herein.

Strategy Training

The Learning Solution

Strategies Included in This Chapter:

✔ The SCORE A Learning Strategy

✔ The Learning Strategies Model

✔ Guidelines for Strategy Training

✔ Developing Your Own Learning Strategies

WHY A STRATEGY TRAINING APPROACH?

As noted in the previous chapter on metacognition, students with learning disabilities demonstrate a variety of organizational problems and can benefit from metacognitive approaches that delineate how they should proceed in accomplishing a specific task. Although mnemonic instruction can facilitate metacognitive planning, a number of researchers advocate more involved training in strategies that are specific to particular learning tasks (Day & Elksnin, 1994; Keeler & Swanson, 2001; Marks, Laeys, Bender, & Scott, 1996; Sousa, 2001b; Vaughn, Gersten, & Chard, 2000) for students with learning disabilities.

For example, consider how the organizational problems of a student with a learning disability, as described previously, may play out when the student is expected to complete a complex assignment such as developing a theme or research paper. To complete this assignment, the student must, at a minimum, select a topic, identify questions/issues within that topic, research each of these (reading and taking lengthy notes), select the appropriate order in which to present these different issues, write a first draft, edit, and then complete a second draft and a final paper. These steps can be quite daunting for the average learner, and for a student with a learning disability, these steps actually prevent the student from accomplishing the task. In short, some type of strategy that spells out these various steps and the order for them is critical. Thus, *strategy training*—some use the term *learning strategy instruction*—for students with learning disabilities was developed, whereby specific strategies (i.e., a set of metaconitive planning and monitoring steps) are developed for specific types of instructional activities (Day & Elksnin, 1994).

What Is a Learning Strategy?

A *learning strategy* is a mnemonic device that assists a student in understanding and completing an academic task, usually by specifying a series of steps to be completed in sequential order (Day & Elksnin, 1994; Marks et al., 1996). Many strategies are summarized in the form of an acronym that the student is expected to memorize and subsequently apply. Although various theorists have developed a variety of strategies to assist students with learning disabilities in metacognitive planning and monitoring of the educational task (Montague, 1992; Montague & Leavell, 1994), much of the early research on strategy training was associated with Dr. Donald Deshler and his coworkers at the University of Kansas Institute for Learning Disabilities (Clark, Deshler, Schumaker, Alley, & Warner, 1984; Deshler, Warner, Schumaker, & Alley, 1984; Ellis, 1994; Ellis, Deshler, & Schumaker, 1989). This early research represents only a small percentage of the growing body of research articles supporting strategy training. This research has indicated that use of learning strategies can create dramatic increases in reading, math, and language arts performance and/or improved performance on many other educational tasks for students with learning disabilities.

More specifically, a learning strategy may be thought of as a method of cognitively planning the performance of a learning task, completing the steps involved in the task, and monitoring completion of the task (Ellis, 1994; Scheid, 1994). As one example, Teaching Tip 4.1 presents a simple learning strategy designed by Korinek and Bulls (1996) that may be used to assist a student with a learning disability in the theme paper assignment described above. By completing the steps designated in this strategy, the student can organize his or her efforts, sequentially complete the correct tasks, and eventually complete the assignment.

The steps in this strategy form a heuristic the student memorizes to complete the task (Korinek & Bulls, 1996). This particular strategy would be used by elementary, middle school, and secondary school students with learning disabilities when a report, a research paper, or a theme paper was assigned in a subject area class. As this example demonstrates, strategy training may be differentiated from a "study skills"

Teaching Tip 4.1

SCORE A: A Research Paper Writing Strategy

Strategy steps include the following:

S   Select a subject

C   Create categories

O   Obtain resources

R   Read and take notes

E   Evenly organize the information

A   Apply the process writing steps

    Planning

    Drafting

    Revising

approach. Whereas study skills include such things as writing down assignments and allocating time for homework, a learning strategy encompasses a metacognitive plan for completing a specific type of school-related task, as well as structuring the inner dialogue of the student to help complete the task.

To date, researchers have produced a large number of strategies (Day & Elksnin, 1994; Deshler et al., 1984; Ellis, 1994; Korinek & Bulls, 1996). These provide insight into various types of tasks, including the following:

- Test-taking skills
- Word identification
- Using pictures in texts
- Chapter assignments in content classes
- Visual imagery to improve comprehension
- Self-questioning
- Searching for answers in text

Some strategies are independent; others include substrategies for various steps (note the substrategies in SCORE A for the writing process itself). Some of the more common learning strategies are presented in Teaching Tip 4.2.

Teaching Tip 4.2:

Common Learning Strategies

RAP	A reading comprehension strategy for checking paragraph comprehension	COPS	An editing strategy for checking a paragraph
R	Read the paragraph	C	Capitalization
A	Ask questions about the content	O	Overall appearance
P	Paraphrase the content	P	Punctuation
		S	Spelling

SCORER	A strategy for taking multiple-choice tests	RIDER	A visual imagery strategy
S	Schedule your time	R	Read the sentence
C	Clue words	I	Imagine a picture of it in your mind
O	Omit difficult questions	D	Describe how the new image differs from the old
R	Read carefully	E	Evaluate to see that the image contains everything
E	Estimate your answer	R	Repeat as you read the next sentence
R	Review your work		

NOTE: Learning strategies are available from a variety of sources (see Bender, 1996; Carman & Adams, 1972; Clark, Deshler, Schumaker, Alley, & Warner, 1984; Day & Elksnin, 1994; Ellis, 1994). Also, the University of Kansas Center for Research on Learning (Lawrence, KS) offers training in strategy instruction.

REFLECTIVE EXERCISE:
TIME TO MASTER A LEARNING STRATEGY

Teachers should select one of the learning strategies presented above and consider how frequently a particular student is likely to use that particular skill during one week in his or her class. For example, the COPS strategy is intended to assist students in editing paragraphs, so teachers should consider how frequently students write paragraphs during the students' "average" week. Next, that number may be multiplied by thirty-six (the number of weeks in a given academic year) and subsequently by ten (the number of years of public schooling after students learn to write

---

☞ **Teaching Tip 4.3**

Steps in Strategy Instruction

1. Pretest and commitment
2. Describe the strategy
3. Model the strategy
4. Verbal rehearsal of the strategy
5. Practice with controlled materials
6. Practice with grade-appropriate materials
7. Commitment to generalize the material
8. Generalization and maintenance

---

paragraphs). This calculation will help almost every teacher justify the time spent in having students master this learning strategy.

USING LEARNING STRATEGIES

Although learning strategies can be used in various ways, Dr. Don Deshler and the other researchers associated with the University of Kansas suggest an eight-step model for instruction in any particular learning strategy, as presented in Teaching Tip 4.3 above. These steps are intended to provide guidance for the teacher in implementing strategic instruction. Also, specific strategy instruction training is provided by the University of Kansas Center for Research on Learning in Lawrence, Kansas. The assumption behind the strategic instruction model is that the special education class will be the setting in which instruction in learning strategies takes place and that strategic applications will then transfer into the general education classroom. In fact, a major strength of this instructional model is that this is one of the few instructional models that specifically addresses the issue of transfer of learning into the general education class. For students with learning disabilities, this strategic instruction can be the single critical component that results in success in the general education class.

Step 1: Pretest and Commitment

First, a student with learning disabilities is tested to determine if he or she needs a strategy for a particular task. The results of the assessment are explained to the student, and the student is informed about the level of performance the new strategy would make possible. A decision is then made involving matching a particular strategy to the task and setting (Day & Elksnin, 1994) and determining whether the student will learn the new strategy. Students should be encouraged to "opt in" to learning the strategy; the learning strategies instructional approach stresses the need for student involvement in this decision and student commitment to the decision to learn a new strategy. This step usually takes one instructional period.

Step 2: Describe the Strategy

During the second step, the strategy is introduced and the various components of the strategy are described to the student. This step focuses on the key elements of the strategy and how these components are used. Also, the student is told where and under what conditions a strategy may be applied. This also usually takes one class period, although the issue of appropriate applications of the strategy will be discussed throughout the course of training.

Step 3: Model the Strategy

On the next day, the teacher models each step of the strategy while discussing the use of the strategy out loud. Thus, the teacher is modeling how a student should give himself or herself verbal instruction (quiet verbal instruction or "inner language") on using the strategy. Each aspect of the strategy is modeled, and students are encouraged to ask questions. This instructional period may include several different tasks, and the teacher may prompt students to model particular aspects of the strategy at various points.

Step 4: Verbal Rehearsal of the Strategy

The expectation for students in this instructional model is that students must learn the strategy by rote; they must state the strategy steps very quickly before they attempt to apply the strategy. The students are also required to identify the action to be taken in each step and tell why each step is important for the strategy overall. This step is intended to facilitate independence in strategy application and can usually be completed by students with learning disabilities in one instructional period.

Step 5: Practice with Controlled Materials

Prior to using the strategy on difficult, grade-level materials, the student should master the application of the strategy on simpler materials;

the assumption behind this step is that the difficulty of the material should not impair the student's ability to learn the strategy. Consequently, the strategy should be applied on "controlled materials" (controlled materials are materials at the student's academic performance level rather than at his or her grade level). If the SCORE A strategy presented in Teaching Tip 4.1 was being taught, the student would first apply that strategy in a two- or three-paragraph theme paper on material that the student had previously mastered. The student would be coached by the teacher using explicit corrective feedback. If a sixth-grade student with a learning disability was completing science work at Grade Level 4, he or she should be given a theme assignment at the fourth-grade level to learn the strategy. A daily record of the student's performance on both the theme and the student's complete and accurate application of the SCORE A strategy would be kept during this step. This step will be repeated over numerous instructional periods involving numerous days of instructional time (perhaps as many as one or two weeks) until the strategy is totally known and completely understood by the student on Grade Level 4 materials. In short, the student must master strategy application at something close to 100% prior to moving on. After the student has demonstrated mastery of the strategy in Grade Level 4 materials, he or she should move on expectations for Grade Level

5, perhaps a four-paragraph themed paper. Also, the student should be encouraged to chart his or her progress on mastery of the learning strategy itself.

Step 6: Practice With Grade-Appropriate Materials

In this instructional model, the level of complexity on which the student practices is gradually increased until the materials approximate those grade-level materials with which the student works. This step also involves the fading out of various prompts and cues the student used in earlier steps. For the student described above, after mastery of the SCORE A strategy on Grade 5 themes, the student would move into expectations for a more complex paper in Grade Level 6. Mastery of the strategy on grade-level materials usually takes between five and ten instructional periods. Again, progress during this phase is charted to present a daily picture of the student's progress.

> The student must master strategy application at something close to 100% prior to moving on.

Step 7: Commitment to Generalize the Strategy

Once the student with a learning disability has mastered the strategy on grade-level materials, the student must be encouraged to see the value of generalizing the new strategy to other similar educational tasks in the general education classroom. A commitment should then be elicited from the student to apply the strategy on all theme-writing assignments in all subject areas. This discussion with the student may take as little as a few minutes during one of the instructional periods, but this commitment to generalize is considered a critical step in the learning process.

Step 8: Generalization and Maintenance

The generalization and maintenance step is, in many ways, the most important aspect of this model. There is little advantage in spending the number of instructional periods discussed above to teach a student the SCORE A strategy unless that student is then taught how to apply that strategy throughout his or her schooling. However, if this strategy is mastered, the student then has a skill that can enhance learning in numerous classes in the future, many of which are dependent on one's ability to successfully write extended themes or reports.

The generalization step involves three phases. The first phase is *orientation to generalization.* This is designed to make the student aware of situations in which the new skill may be tried. The student is encouraged to make adaptions of the original strategy for various types of tests. The second phase is *activation,* where the student is given specific assignments to apply the strategy in grade-appropriate materials from other general education classes. Throughout this process, the special education teacher is encouraged to work with the general education teacher in encouraging use of the strategy. The teacher then checks the output of the strategy.

Finally, a *maintenance* phase is implemented. The students who have been trained in a particular strategy should be periodically reminded to use that strategy, and the teacher should check the work output when the strategy is applied.

> The generalization and maintenance step is, in many ways, the most important aspect of this model.

📖 REFLECTIVE EXERCISE: INSTRUCTIONAL CROSS-FERTILIZATION AND THE REFLECTIVE TEACHER

Reflect for a moment on the quality of the instructional strategies recommended in this eight-step instructional plan. What ideas can you identify that are presented here and have been suggested previously in this text (e.g., students taking responsibility for their learning; modeling)? Why do differentiated instructional strategies that stem from different theoretical models tend to emphasize many of the same instructional techniques?

A STRATEGY TRAINING EXAMPLE

Although the descriptions of strategy instruction herein involve a joint effort between a special educator and a general educator, there is no reason why a single teacher—either in general education or special education—cannot apply strategy instruction. Furthermore, a number of authors have provided suggestions for implementing strategy training by any teacher who wishes to do so (Day & Elksnin, 1994; Marks et al., 1996). Consideration of the teaching tips provided by Day and Elksnin (1994) should help the teacher walk through the following application example.

With these instructional suggestions in mind, review the following strategy instruction example. RAP is a strategy for paraphrasing reading material that was presented in Teaching Tip 4.2. This was one of the first strategies developed and is applicable from the lower grades up through secondary school. The next section of the text traces the implementation of this strategy over a period of thirty-five school days to give a specific, hands-on example of strategy instruction. Again, although this example

☞ **Teaching Tip 4.4**

Using Strategy Instruction

1. Choose a strategy that matches a task or setting demand for the student.

2. Assess the students' current level of strategy use and teach a strategy that is needed to increase their level of performance.

3. Have students set goals about what they intend to learn and how they will use the strategy.

4. Describe the strategy, give examples, and discuss its applications.

5. Model the strategy for the students. Verbalize your own thinking and problem solving, including ways you monitor, make corrections, and adjust your task approach and completion.

6. Make sure students can confidently name and explain the strategy.

7. Give sufficient practice of the strategy with materials that are controlled for level of difficulty before expecting use of the strategy in advanced materials.

8. Have students practice the strategy in materials from classes in which they are placed for instruction.

9. Make sure students give examples and actually practice the strategy in various settings in school, at home, and in the community.

SOURCE: From "Promoting Strategic Learning," by Day, V. P., & Elksnin, L. K. (1994). *Intervention in School and Clinic, 29,* 262-270. ©1994 by PRO-ED, Inc. Used with permission.

---

involves application of the strategy as a team effort, every teacher in the classroom today should be employing strategy instruction for students with learning disabilities, regardless of the opportunity for a team effort. The extant research on strategy instruction strongly supports that bold statement (Day & Elksnin, 1994; Deshler et al., 1984; Ellis, 1994; Ellis et al., 1989; Korinek & Bulls, 1996; Vaughn et al., 2000).

Let's assume that the special education teacher, Mr. Langone, has three students with learning disabilities in an inclusive eighth-grade classroom during the first period of each day. Ms. Rooten is the general education teacher for that class, which also includes twenty-two students without disabilities. The reading level of the students with learning disabilities ranges from Grade Level 4 to 5, and independent of these three students, the reading level for the entire inclusive class ranges from Level 5 up through Level 11—in short, the typical reading variation in a general education classroom.

On the first day, after Ms. Rooten and Mr. Langone decide to use the RAP strategy for the three students with learning disabilities, Mr. Langone gives out prepared readings of five paragraphs for each student with learning disabilities at the student's grade placement. He tells the students that they are to read their paragraphs silently and then record (on a cassette recorder) what they have read. He reminds the students that they will be tested on the material the next day. Overnight, he will score the audiotapes on "story reading points" (i.e., the main idea and up to two supporting details from each paragraph are each worth 1 point if the student noted them, and the points are then totaled to get a reading score). This becomes one of the students' pretest scores.

On the second day, Mr. Langone administers an individual comprehension test, perhaps ten questions, on the passage each student previously read. The percentage of correct responses becomes the comprehension score for that student on that story. Also, on the second day, the test results are communicated to each student to demonstrate the need for a new strategy for reading comprehension. At this point, the student is asked if he or she would like to learn a new strategy to help better remember what has been read. The student should then write a long-term goal stating this commitment. Also, a management chart that records daily performance on both RAP reading points and reading comprehension is initiated for each student.

> Every teacher in the classroom today should be employing strategy instruction for students with learning disabilities.

The lesson on the next day is a description of the strategy. Using a cue card that displays the steps of the strategy, Mr. Langone will first discuss the meaning of paraphrasing and the use of this skill in various subjects. He may include both students with disabilities and students without disabilities in this segment of the instruction. He will point out the advantages of the ability to paraphrase in terms of increased comprehension. Students are then encouraged to set goals for learning the strategy, with a suggested guideline provided by the teacher. Mr. Langone will then discuss the strategy steps in order, carefully giving the students examples. First, reading is discussed, as attending to the meaning of the words. Second, several ways to find the main idea (such as looking for repetitive words in the paragraph or studying the first sentence) and details from the paragraph are provided. Next, the need to put the ideas into the student's own words is discussed. Finally, the criteria for a good paraphrase are presented to the students so that they know how their work will be graded.

The fourth day provides the opportunity for the teacher to model the strategy. Mr. Langone will read an appropriate passage of five paragraphs and implement the RAP strategy. Before starting, he will verbally remind himself of the strategy, thus modeling self-instruction in this strategy. He will then read the passage aloud and discuss the strategy with himself. "Now that I have read the first paragraph, I have to list the main idea and some details." After several ideas are specified, Mr. Langone will put these on tape, in his own words. This is done for the first several paragraphs, and students are involved in the last several paraphrasing attempts.

The next day is spent on verbal practice of the components of the strategy. Each student should be able to name the series of steps from memory and provide information on how to complete each step. With a cue card in front of the class that summarizes the steps, the students should be encouraged to state the next step of the strategy or to answer any question Mr. Langone asks. For example, they should be able to give at least two suggestions for finding the main idea of a paragraph.

> The criteria for a good paraphrase are presented to the students so that they know how their work will be graded.

The next day begins the controlled practice for the paraphrasing strategy. Each of the three students is given a five-paragraph reading at the student's independent reading level—the level at which a student has 95% mastery of the words (that reading level will typically be several grade levels below the grade-level placement for students with learning disabilities). First, Mr. Langone briefly reviews the steps in the strategy with the students. Then, the students are told to use the RAP strategy with each paragraph, recording one main idea and two major details for each.

The RAP reading worksheets presented in Teaching Tip 4.5 may be used for this paraphrasing exercise, and these are scored using the same criteria as the pretest. Depending on the time, the students may also take the comprehension test for that reading selection. Mr. Langone also has the option of using the class period on the next day as a comprehension test day. The comprehension test typically is a ten-question test on the reading passage. That quiz, coupled with the score on the RAP reading worksheet, can provide a very good indication of students' overall comprehension performance. Thus, the student completes a RAP reading worksheet and a comprehension test for each five-paragraph passage read, and each of these scores is placed on the student's individual progress chart.

The scoring of student work on both the paraphrase worksheet and the comprehension test for each reading selection should be used as an opportunity to provide corrective and positive feedback. Frequent feedback is a critical component of learning for students with learning disabilities, and this instructional method facilitates such feedback. To provide appropriate feedback, Mr. Langone will identify several things that each student did well and share these with the student. Also, he will

👉 Teaching Tip 4.5

A RAP Worksheet

For each paragraph in the five-paragraph reading passage, the student should list the main idea and two supporting details in the space provided below.

1. Main Idea _____

    Detail 1: _____

    Detail 2: _____

2. Main Idea _____

    Detail 1: _____

    Detail 2: _____

3. Main Idea _____

    Detail 1: _____

    Detail 2: _____

4. Main Idea _____

    Detail 1: _____

    Detail 2: _____

5. Main Idea _____

    Detail 1: _____

    Detail 2: _____

review the requirements that were not met when a student did not receive credit for an answer on the RAP reading worksheet or the comprehension test. After both a RAP reading worksheet and a comprehension test are completed on a five-paragraph reading segment, the student will read another reading selection at the same grade level. This series of daily lessons is continued until the student reaches mastery level in both paraphrasing and comprehension of the material at that grade level. On average, students may be expected to reach mastery of this step in three to six practice attempts at each grade level, though some students with learning disabilities may take longer. Thus, if a student's reading level is Grade 4, and the student is in an eighth-grade general education classroom, he or she may take up to twenty-four days to achieve mastery at grade-level work in Grades 4, 5, 6, and 7, respectively.

> Frequent feedback is a critical component of learning for students with learning disabilities, and this instructional method facilitates such feedback.

The next step emphasizes grade-appropriate practice for the student, and the students will, in all probability, reach this step on different days. The student will then be given grade-appropriate materials at his or her grade level and will practice until mastery is achieved. His or her final passage should be taken from a text that is normally used at his or her grade level.

The next step involves the posttest and student commitment to generalize the strategy. The student (we'll call him John) will complete a paraphrase task and a comprehension test for a passage that consists of five paragraphs of reading from his grade placement level. Results of these will be noted on the progress chart. Mr. Langone will discuss the entire learning procedure with John to point out the progress depicted in the chart. He will then obtain a commitment from John to generalize the strategy to other textbooks in the general education classroom. This step takes only one instructional period, but the commitment step must be done with each student individually and is critical for students with learning disabilities.

The next day, Mr. Langone begins the final step with John—generalization. John is asked to use his textbook and Mr. Langone gathers reading material from other settings, such as the home, newspapers, magazines that interest John, and so forth. Mr. Langone will discuss with John the use of each book and material. At this stage, Ms. Rooten—the general education teacher—should become involved by meeting with John and Mr. Langone to discuss strategy application in the materials from the inclusive general education classroom. John will make cue cards for the strategy and tape these inside the front of each textbook, and other cues for using the strategy are discussed. Ms. Rooten will make an agreement with John to remind him to use the RAP strategy whenever appropriate on a reading assignment.

The next day begins the activation phase of the generalization step. Mr. Langone will present a "Report of Strategy Use" form that consists of a series of lines on which John will enter each use of the strategy from the general education classes. The form also lists the date and the type of material on which the strategy was used: textbook, newspaper, novel, or magazine. Mr. Langone will generate various assignments from these reading materials for the student to complete sometime within the next twenty-four hours. These are quickly graded by Mr. Langone or Ms. Rooten, and corrective feedback is given where necessary. The student should complete six different activities of this nature. Mr. Langone will also discuss the completion of the form for particular dates, and John will keep a record for a two-week period on utilization of the strategy.

Maintenance is the last phase of the generalization step. This consists of a series of evaluations similar to the posttest; these are generally done one week after the student completes the activation phase. At this point, John has internalized a strategy that should facilitate his reading comprehension across grade levels and for all types of reading materials. Of course, both Ms. Rooten and Mr. Langone should frequently remind John to perform the strategy on appropriate work in John's various classes.

As can be seen, the example above uses a number of methods that are the hallmark of differentiated instruction, including modeling, scaffolds for memorizing the task (e.g., RAP), use of inner language, corrective and timely feedback, and repeated guided practice. Use of effective teaching behaviors greatly enhances the efficacy of the learning strategies model of instruction. Again, the research on strategic instruction is so strongly supportive that every teacher of students with learning disabilities should be implementing this method for tasks that give particular students problems.

> The commitment step must be done with each student individually and is critical for students with learning disabilities.

Although the example above presented the ideal collaboration between a general education and a special education teacher, general education teachers who do not have a collaborative relationship with a special educator should also consider implementing this learning strategies instructional approach. Of course, this may be a bit more difficult for a single teacher to implement, the results of modifying the learning process through strategic instruction will greatly increase the learning level within the general education class.

👉 **Teaching Tip 4.6**

Developing Task Specific Strategies

1. Specify the type of task that the strategy is designed to facilitate. Identify a task that will yield a daily performance measure, so that you may chart the progress of the student.

2. Describe the task in sequential order. Students should be able to use the task acronym not only as a memory tool to remember the steps but also as an organizational tool that presents the steps in the task in sequence.

3. Summarize each step. You should write a brief statement that summarizes each step in the sequence, with precise and concise instructions for the student.

4. Limit the strategy. You should limit the strategy to a specific type of task. Think of examples and nonexamples that you can use to illustrate for the student when to use or not use the strategy.

5. Develop a mnemonic acronym to assist the student in memorizing the sequential steps in the strategy. Creativity will play a part here, and some license may be used. Still, you should phrase the acronym such that the most important work (usually the verb) in the step is emphasized in the acronym.

SOURCE: Summarized from Marks, Laeys, Bender, & Scott (1996).

DEVELOPING YOUR OWN STRATEGIES

Although specific training in strategic instruction provides the best preparation for implementation of this instructional method (for the availability of summer institute training, you may wish to contact the Department of Special Education at the University of Kansas, Lawrence, KS), teachers can and should implement strategic instruction based on the information available to them. Furthermore, rather than merely apply strategies that are presented in this chapter or other available literature, many teachers have begun to develop specific learning strategies for use in their own classrooms (Ellis et al., 1989; Marks et al., 1996). The steps suggested by Marks et al. (1996) and presented in Teaching Tip 4.6 should help you in developing strategies specific to the needs of your students.

As one example, one veteran teacher in a special education classroom noted that several of her students needed assistance in interpreting information from pictures in their reading material, and she developed the AIDE strategy, presented in Teaching Tip 4.7 above. Every veteran

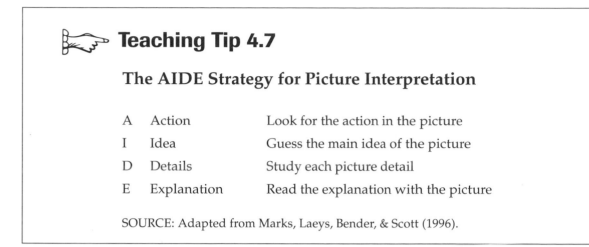

teacher realizes that much of the information presented in pictures and picture captions in various texts may not be presented in the text sections of the chapter. However, this information may very well appear on the end of chapter test. Thus, students with learning disabilities should be taught a specific strategy to glean information from pictures and picture captions in text.

The teacher printed the AIDE strategy on a task card that was presented to the students each day. Also presented each day were three picture cards that each student had to interpret. Students were told to use the AIDE strategy with each picture and were then presented with a ten-question comprehension test on the three pictures. A multiple baseline research project demonstrated that this procedure worked quite well in assisting students with disabilities to focus on the information contained in pictures. Furthermore, this illustrates differentiated instruction, based on a teacher noting a specific need on the part of one or more of the students and addressing that with a strategic instructional approach.

CONCLUSION

The use of strategic instruction for students with learning disabilities is as strongly supported by research as any available instructional technique (Vaughn et al., 2000). Furthermore, the research has likewise demonstrated that this technique (like many others described in this book) works quite well for a large number of other students in the general education classroom also. As a response to this powerful research, I can truthfully suggest that every teacher in general education should employ some type of strategic instruction for his or her students with learning disabilities.

What's Next?

The last several chapters have provided a solid set of differentiated instructional ideas that can enhance learning in any classroom in almost any subject area. With these ideas as the background, the next chapter will present suggestions for modification of the instructional process via modification of instructional groupings. Specifically, several options for peer tutoring will be explored.

5

Tutoring in the Inclusive Classroom

Differentiating Instruction and Increasing Instructional Time

CECIL FORE III
WILLIAM N. BENDER

Strategies Included in This Chapter:

✔ Decisions in Beginning Tutoring

✔ Instructional Plan for Tutor Training

✔ Checklist for Initiating a Tutoring System

✔ Classwide Peer Tutoring (CWPT)

✔ Peer-Assisted Learning Strategies (PALS)

Students with learning disabilities often make significant demands on the teacher's time. Because of their noted problems with attention skills, these students need examples explained many more times than nondisabled learners and generally seem to require assistance more than other students. They also need to be reminded to return to task, or they are disciplined for unruly behavior more frequently. In the differentiated classroom, the teacher must address all of these needs for students with disabilities. For this reason, it is not uncommon for teachers to feel overwhelmed when three or four students with learning disabilities are in their general education classroom. Teachers often feel that there is simply not enough time to do effective instruction for many students with learning disabilities. Furthermore, when considering differentiating the instruction based on the needs of learners with learning disabilities (LD), teachers may simply feel there are not enough hours in the day to accomplish these many instructional tasks.

For these reasons, numerous researchers and practitioners have recommended peer tutoring as one innovative instructional procedure that increases instructional time for students with learning disabilities while reducing the time that the teacher has to spend with each student (Bender, 1996; Fulk & King, 2001; Greenwood, 1991; Maheady, Harper, & Sacca, 1988; Mortweet, Utley, Walker, Dawson, Delquadri, Reddy, & Greenwood, 1999). In short, students can and do learn from each other—in many cases, students learn better from each other than they do when instructed by a teacher. Furthermore, with appropriate instructional scaffolds (e.g., in the form of a set of instructions for modeling a learning task), students can teach other students and still benefit from the teacher's expertise. For this reason, the wise general education teacher will take advantage of the peer tutoring option for increasing instructional time. Thus, peer tutoring, in some form, is one critical instructional skill for the differentiated classroom that every teacher should have as an option in the general education class.

Research has demonstrated quite strongly that peer tutoring is one effective method by which students with various disabilities may be successfully integrated into inclusive general education classrooms (Fuchs et al., 2001; Maheady et al., 1988). For example, in one study, Carlson, Litton, and Zinkgraf (1985) investigated the effectiveness of peer tutoring in word recognition tasks among children with mild intellectual disabilities (we describe this study in this context because studies of peer tutoring using exclusively groups with learning disabilities are limited). Twelve classes were used, and six of these were randomly selected as the experimental group. These experimental classes included seventy-four students, and the other six classes (with sixty-two students) became the control group. A statistical comparison demonstrated that these two groups were comparable in reading ability before the experiment began. In the experimental group, the students were assigned the role of tutor or tutee based on their pretest reading score, with the higher-scoring students assigned the role of tutor. These tutors were then instructed in conducting a flash-card drill activity to assist their tutees in learning unknown words. The students in the control group were instructed by the teacher in the traditional fashion. Results demonstrated that both the tutors and tutees learned more words during the instructional phase than the students in the six control classes. Also, statistical comparison revealed that both the tutors and tutees in the experimental group made significant gains in reading comprehension as a result of the peer tutoring instructional activities. Additional research on efficacy will be presented later in this chapter, and although not all of the research is

Peer tutoring works!

supportive of tutoring, the bulk of the research is supportive, and when the time demands of an inclusive class are considered, the research does suggest that this instructional method should be used in almost every classroom in our nation's schools.

INITIATING A PEER TUTORING SYSTEM

REFLECTIVE ACTIVITY: PREDICTING THE ISSUES IN INITIATING A PEER TUTORING SYSTEM

As a reflective activity, jot down a series of notes on the decisions involved in initiating a peer tutoring system in your class. What types of things will have to be considered in advance? After listing a series of issues and concerns, compare your notes with the issues noted below.

Tutoring systems are relatively easy to initiate (Fuchs et al., 2001; Fulk & King, 2001), although certain tutoring systems require more time than others. Also, there are several specific decisions to make before you start. These are summarized in Teaching Tip 5.1.

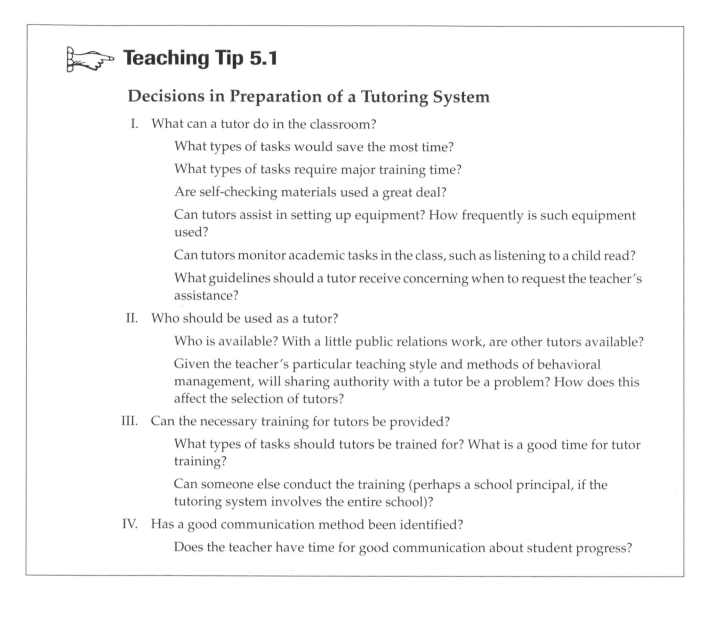

Teaching Tip 5.1

Decisions in Preparation of a Tutoring System

I. What can a tutor do in the classroom?

What types of tasks would save the most time?

What types of tasks require major training time?

Are self-checking materials used a great deal?

Can tutors assist in setting up equipment? How frequently is such equipment used?

Can tutors monitor academic tasks in the class, such as listening to a child read?

What guidelines should a tutor receive concerning when to request the teacher's assistance?

II. Who should be used as a tutor?

Who is available? With a little public relations work, are other tutors available?

Given the teacher's particular teaching style and methods of behavioral management, will sharing authority with a tutor be a problem? How does this affect the selection of tutors?

III. Can the necessary training for tutors be provided?

What types of tasks should tutors be trained for? What is a good time for tutor training?

Can someone else conduct the training (perhaps a school principal, if the tutoring system involves the entire school)?

IV. Has a good communication method been identified?

Does the teacher have time for good communication about student progress?

What a Peer Tutor Can Do

The first consideration in initiating a tutoring system is delineating the specific tasks for the student tutor to accomplish. It may be helpful to think of the various tasks in terms of different levels, depending on the degree of complexity of the tutoring assignment and the instructional skills a person should have before attempting to teach a particular task to a student with learning disabilities. For example, with very little preparation, almost any peer tutor can enter the inclusive class and begin to assist in checking a student's objective answers on a worksheet, particularly if an answer sheet is provided. However, if the teacher wants a student to assist with reading comprehension questioning exercises or lead a prereading discussion using an advance organizer for a story, some training may be necessary. Clearly, the types of tasks required from a tutor will affect the training the tutor requires, and considering these tasks as different tutoring levels should assist in the decisions about what particular peer tutors can do.

The teacher must take the final responsibility for deciding what the peer tutors do in the class. Teachers may consider the types of activities typically done that do not require complex instruction, and peer tutors can begin those tasks immediately. The list of simple peer tutoring tasks may include the following:

> The first consideration in initiating a tutoring system is delineating the specific tasks for the student tutor to accomplish.

- Checking student worksheets
- Rechecking the self-checking worksheets students complete
- Listening to oral reading and correcting oral reading errors
- Assisting with dictionary skills
- Monitoring group art projects

Each of these activities (and many others) can be accomplished with very little training for the tutor. For our purposes in this text, these tasks will be considered Level 1 tasks because these require very little (if any) preparation on the part of the tutor.

However, certain activities require more training. These activities may include assisting a student with comprehension of a math problem, using an advanced organizer to assist in reading comprehension, or offering reinforcement for completed work. Because these skills are more complex, teachers will want the tutor to learn how to accomplish them prior to using the tutor to instruct other students. Still, training in these skills can be as simple as having the new peer tutor observe while the teacher works with a student on one of these tasks, and in most cases, very little out-of-class instructional time will be necessary in training tutors for these tasks. This type of task is referred to as a Level 2 task; some training is necessary, which is generally conducted during "in-class" time and involves modeling the tutoring for the tutor and discussing it with him or her.

Next, certain tasks may require some training outside of class, and these may be considered Level 3 tasks. Examples would include implementation of a learning strategies curriculum or assisting students in completing self-management behavioral charts on their own performance. The specific training associated with these tasks is described throughout the remainder of this chapter.

Finally, there are certain types of instructional tasks that only the teacher should perform. These are referred to as Level 4 tasks and are some of the more difficult decision-making tasks involved in teaching. These tasks, if done incorrectly, may have a very negative impact on the student's development, and for this reason, these tasks should be completed only by the teacher. These Level 4 tasks would include such things as providing initial instruction on a new type of math problem, punishing students for misbehavior, or planning the next set of instructional activities for the students.

Clearly, when contemplating a tutoring system, teachers must consider the level of task the tutor will perform; teachers must then make time for the appropriate training for the peer tutors. For Level 3 tasks in particular, training can be critical to the success of the peer tutoring efforts, and nothing positive will be gained if the teacher begins to use peer tutors for complex tasks for which the tutors have received no training.

Who Should Be a Peer Tutor?

Tutors may be obtained from any number of sources, including the teacher's class, the school, or other schools on the same campus. As one example, many teachers obtain peer tutors by inquiring in the scheduling office about having two or three study hall students who may wish to serve as tutors assigned to the class. The guidance counselor can often identify several students who would be willing to serve as a tutor for a semester. These students would then begin to assist with Level 1 tasks immediately, and, with a few training observations, they may also begin to assist in Level 2 tasks.

Research has also demonstrated the effectiveness of having students with learning disabilities tutor other students with or without disabilities (Fulk & King, 2001; Top & Osguthorpe, 1987). Thus, in either a general education class or in a special education class, one potential supply of peer tutors is in the class. Using this resource pool of potential tutors, the teacher's initial exploration with tutoring may be as simple as an individual, single assignment tutoring experience—that is, using one student to assist another student on a single assignment in class. Many teachers feel more comfortable beginning in this limited fashion and then expanding their tutoring program to more students and more complex assignments. Of course, this can easily grow into an exercise for the entire class, and later in this chapter we will describe several plans for using the entire class in tutoring.

With these potential tutoring sources noted, tutoring seems to become more feasible for almost any classroom today. Thus, if you wish to differentiate the instruction in your classroom, and some type of tutoring system is not in place, you should consider starting one. The simplest method is to use students in the class to tutor others. Although using students with learning disabilities as tutors has been supported by research, this type of tutoring system requires more active monitoring of the tutor-tutee interactions (Fulk & King, 2001; Maher 1982, 1984; Scruggs, Mastropieri, Veit, & Osguthorpe, 1986). Still, with very little training, students with learning disabilities can assist others in the class, and this holds many benefits for students with learning disabilities in areas such as self-concept enhancement and improved peer interactions. Obviously, although almost any student can successfully manage Level 1 tasks, prior to assigning a peer tutor to Level 2 or Level 3 tasks, teachers should train the tutors to ensure that the student knows the material and the instructional tutoring method in the proposed lesson completely.

> Some tasks, if done incorrectly, may have a very negative impact on the student's development, and for this reason, these tasks should be completed only by the teacher.

Teachers should also consider the gender of the tutor-tutee pairs. At certain ages (generally Grades 1 through 5—the early years through the puberty years), children of opposite sexes do not mix a great deal socially, and teachers may want to use only male tutors with male students and female tutors with female students. Beyond that age, gender should still be considered (i.e., be cognizant of who is dating or friends with whom), but it is quite permissible to use students of a different gender as tutors if the teacher feels that the pairing will be beneficial. Furthermore, the teacher will need to consider the social acceptance of each student in the proposed tutoring pair. Teachers should pair students together who have some history of working together, if at all possible. Tutors selected on this basis can begin to assist in Level 1 tasks immediately. One word of caution is in order. The teacher will have to maintain complete control over the tutoring system and may have to discipline the tutors discretely if they begin to misbehave in the tutoring situation or to overstep the responsibilities of tutoring.

One critical concern in tutoring programs that must be emphasized for tutors in every level of tutoring is the requirement for confidentiality. Tutors must understand that they should never discuss a student's work outside the context of the class, nor is it ever appropriate to poke fun at students for mistakes on work during a tutoring session. Some teachers develop a "tutoring contract" that the tutors are requested to sign prior to participating in the tutoring. That contract should include the expectations of the tutoring, the length of the tutoring commitment (the second author of this chapter used a one grading period commitment in the tutoring contract), and a privacy/confidentiality provision.

If students are unwilling to sign and abide by this contract, other tutors should be found.

Training the Tutors

As noted previously, the task level assigned to tutors has a direct bearing on the types of training that must be provided. Level 1 tasks can be assigned to any tutor on the first day of tutoring, whereas Level 3 tasks may require complicated training. For implementing a peer tutoring option, there are at least three training choices. First, one observation combined with a critical review/debriefing session may be enough of a training process for many peer tutors in Level 2 tasks. This generally involves merely having the student observe the teacher while tutoring another child once or perhaps twice. On each occasion, the teacher should debrief the tutor to ensure that he or she understands the role. Delquadri, Greenwood, Whorton, Carta, and Hall (1986) recommended this type of training.

> One critical concern in tutoring programs that must be emphasized for tutors in every level of tutoring is the requirement for confidentiality.

A more involved level of training for Level 3 tasks actually involves some outside-of-class time. For a tutor to be of benefit in conducting an advanced organizer lesson for a reading assignment, as one example, the tutor may be required merely to watch for several days as the teacher works through an advance organizer prior to having students read the assigned material. The teacher can then discuss the concept of the advance organizer with the tutor after class, answering any questions concerning the use of such an organizer as a prereading activity. Finally, the teacher may wish to role-play with the prospective tutor, having the peer tutor "teach" using an advance organizer. Afterward, the teacher would debrief the student and critique his or her performance. The advantage of this type of training is that the peer tutor would be able to conduct more involved lessons than tutors with less training.

The highest level of tutor training involves extended extra-class training. For example, for a tutor to understand the purpose of a learning strategies instructional method, the teacher may require the tutor to read certain materials on learning strategies prior to conducting observations of teaching sessions or role-play activities. Also, extra-class time may be needed to go over these materials with the peer tutor before he or she is considered ready to observe a learning strategies lesson in your class. Much of the research on tutoring has used models of tutor training that require extra-class training time during the initial stages (Fuchs et al., 2001; Lazerson, Foster, Brown, & Hummel, 1988; Russell & Ford, 1984). For example, Russell and Ford (1984) trained tutors during a three-hour training session prior to implementation of the tutoring program. Beirne-Smith (1991) used a more involved tutor training to prepare tutors to teach math to students with learning disabilities. She had two instructional sessions of forty-five minutes each, during which tutors were trained in two different instructional methods. Clearly, the level of task you want tutors to perform will determine the type and extent of necessary training, with Level 2 tasks and Level 3 tasks requiring much more training.

Finally, if extensive training of tutors for Level 3 tasks is necessary, you should prepare a set of detailed written instructions for the tutors to follow to ensure that their instructional presentation is standardized. This type of lesson format may be an appropriate choice for you in preparing the instructional session for your peer tutors to conduct. There are numerous examples in the literature of scripted lessons for tutors. Teaching Tip 5.2 presents a set of instructions for tutors that Beirne-Smith (1991) used in tutor training.

Communication With the Tutor

If the tutors are merely conducting Level 1 tasks, there is very little need for structured communication concerning student progress because the tutees' progress is typically represented in the form of some corrected worksheet or score sheet on some activity. These tutors merely do the types of activities identified by the teacher, and these suggestions are generally made while class is in progress. However, not all work results in a worksheet, and thus, for some peer tutoring activities, teachers should construct the tutoring lessons specifically to require a permanent product (i.e., a written record) of the student's performance on the task, such as collection of the worksheet the tutor has graded. This allows the teacher to monitor the student's progress and plan the student's instruction appropriately.

> The task level assigned to tutors has a direct bearing on the types of training that must be provided.

However, in situations where the tutor is trained to conduct instructional Level 2 and Level 3 tasks (or in inclusive classes where two or more teachers may direct the tutor), additional and more structured communication about the student's progress may be necessary. For example, many teachers assign a particular time slot to the tutor each day for conducting an instructional assignment with a student (e.g., during the first fifteen minutes of the period each day, the tutor may be expected to work with Billy on spelling exercises). Clearly, some form of daily communication between the peer tutor and the teachers regarding Billy's performance is necessary. One option is to require a brief written summary each day—usually a single paragraph—that summarizes the

☞ **Teaching Tip 5.2**

Instructional Session Plan for Tutor Training

In the Beirne-Smith (1991) study, students with learning disabilities received tutoring in addition facts from older students without learning disabilities. Training in math facts was based on twenty sets of three "related" math facts in which the first addend in each set was held constant and the second addend was increased by 1 (e.g., $2 + 4 = 6$; $2 + 5 = 7$; $2 + 6 = 8$). For each set, a file folder was prepared showing the math facts without the answer on the front and the math facts with the answer on the back. With materials prepared in that fashion, the following task instructions were provided.

The tutor should display the file with answers, point to second addends and sums, and follow the steps below.

1. Rule stating (e.g., "Each time the addend increases by 1 the sum increases by 1. Say it with me.")

2. Demonstration (e.g., "My turn, $2 + 4 = 6$; $2 + 5 = 7$; $2 + 6 = 8$.")

3. Unison responding (e.g., "Say it with me: $2 + 4 = \ldots$.")

4. Individual turns ("Say it by yourself.")

5. Testing ("Say it again" while showing the file without answers.)

This type of task card, prepared for the instructional situations in which you expect your tutor to function (Level 2 or Level 3), will facilitate effective instruction.

SOURCE: Adapted from Beirne-Smith (1991).

lesson and notes the number and types of errors made during the day. This would be turned in to the teacher in addition to copies of the student's worksheets.

As a final option for Level 2 and Level 3 tutoring tasks, many researchers recommend some type of daily performance chart (Greenwood, 1991; Maheady et al., 1988; Mortweet, Utley, Walker, Dawson, Delquadri, Reddy, & Greenwood, 1999). Charting students' performance is often very helpful, and for many kids, the chart itself begins to serve as a reinforcer for successful performance. For this reason, almost every peer tutoring research demonstration has emphasized the use of charted performance measures for each tutoring session each day. In any case, it should be stressed to all concerned that the teacher is responsible for the instruction in his or her class and needs to be fully informed of student progress, and some communication format will need to be in place to fully inform teachers of their students' progress.

Putting the Tutoring System Together

The four major concerns discussed earlier will be the basis of success or failure of your tutoring program: who will do the tutoring, tasks of the tutors, tutor training, and communication with the tutor. Of course these issues are all interrelated, and once the teacher decides on these factors, the peer tutoring strategy is ready. The steps in initiating a tutoring system are presented in Teaching Tip 5.3.

These steps are based on a tutoring system in which other students from the school (i.e., not in the teacher's class) are to be used as tutors. This tutoring system is a bit more complex to initiate; thus, if teachers can accomplish this, they will easily be able to initiate a peer tutoring system by using tutors from their own class. Also, most of these recommendations are generally appropriate during the initiation of each type of tutoring system.

First, permissions should be obtained from the administrators, including the school principal and, perhaps, the director of special education in your district. Teachers may wish to share some research articles or reviews of the literature (cited throughout this chapter) on the effectiveness of using peer tutoring for students with disabilities.

In particular, one fear concerning peer tutoring is the possibility of wasting the time of the tutors, and this concern must be addressed. Not only will other teachers express this fear, but many parents of the tutors may share this concern! Of course, the research on peer tutoring will lay this fear to rest. The research demonstrates that a tutoring program is usually quite beneficial for all persons involved; specifically, both the tutors and tutees learn better and develop better attitudes toward academic work, and those results have been demonstrated repeatedly over the years (Beirne-Smith, 1991; Fulk & King, 2001; Greenwood, 1991; Maheady et al., 1988; Sasso, Mitchell, & Struthers, 1986; Scruggs & Richter, 1985).

Second, teachers should involve the school guidance counselor to discuss the students who may become tutors. For example, this person may be able to identify any students with potential behavior problems among the pool of potential tutors. Likewise, the guidance counselor will be able to identify students who may make very effective tutors. If your school has a "Future Teachers of America" club or similar organizations, teachers should select potential tutors from those organizations by going to a meeting and asking for volunteers.

Third, teachers should identify more tutors than they can initially use. This will provide a pool of prospective tutors. Then the teacher should meet with the prospective tutors themselves, explain the

☞ Teaching Tip 5.3

Checklist for Initiating a Tutoring System

Permissions

___ Obtain permission from school administrators.

___ Obtain permission from each prospective tutor's parents.

Tutor selection

___ Identify time slots when tutors are needed.

___ Request that the guidance counselor suggest some tutors.

___ Request recommendations and support from other teachers.

Meeting with tutors

___ Discuss your needs from tutors.

___ Outline the prospective duties and privileges of tutors.

___ Elicit a commitment from tutors for one grading period.

___ Verify each student's parental permission.

Begin tutoring system

___ Have student observe in each task for which he or she will be used.

___ Observe the tutor while he or she conducts a tutoring session.

___ Tutors begin to conduct the sessions themselves.

Initiation of tutor training

___ Identify which Level 2 or Level 3 tasks you wish to have tutors conduct.

___ Identify the tutors whom you think capable of conducting these tasks.

___ Identify method of training (reading, modeling, videotapes).

___ Begin in-class training after the tutor completes tasks.

Students hand out papers and help in many ways.

proposed tutoring job and responsibilities, and elicit their cooperation. After hearing about the program, some tutors may choose not to participate, and this is fine if teachers have initially selected more than enough. Tutors should sign an agreement to act as tutors for at least one grading period, and every student tutor should have the option of leaving the tutoring program at that time. At this point, the teacher would then send a parental permission letter home to the parents of the tutors, explaining the system, the time involvement of the tutors, and the advantages of tutoring. For tutoring applications that are not reciprocal in nature (such as the tutoring described thus far in this chapter), teachers should use students as tutors only after parental permission has been obtained.

Fourth, begin the tutoring responsibilities with Level 1 tasks on the first day of tutoring. Generally, all students in schools can check a paper when an answer key is provided. These Level 1 tasks from the first week of the tutoring program let the teacher observe the tutors and their relationships with the students with learning disabilities in your class. At this point, the teacher will have the option of using some tutors exclusively for Level 1 tasks and selecting other tutors for more involved training for Level 2 and Level 3 tasks. These decisions may be made through observation of the tutors in their early tutoring experiences. On rare occasions, teachers may have to counsel some student tutors to withdraw from the tutoring program, explaining that not everyone has the personality to be a teacher or tutor. However, this should be a fairly rare occurrence.

Finally, after the teacher determines which students to use for more complex tasks, the teacher may approach them and inquire about a year-long commitment; there is little reason to provide extensive tutor training for tutors who may choose to leave the tutoring experience after only one grading period. After several tutors indicate a desire to continue

> There is little reason to provide extensive tutor training for tutors who may choose to leave the tutoring experience after only one grading period.

over a longer time period, a more extensive training session may be designed to prepare those tutors for monitoring of comprehension through the use of advanced organizers and other complex instructional strategies. As discussed previously, teachers may use some combination of modeling the lesson format, required readings, and scripted lessons as the basis for your training.

CLASSWIDE PEER TUTORING (CWPT)

Peer tutoring is one of the most effective tactics available to assist students with learning disabilities in the differentiated classroom and can increase the quality and amount of instruction that students with learning disabilities receive. Furthermore, research has been strongly supportive of peer tutoring in terms of positive results for both tutors and tutees. For these reasons, tutoring has received increasing research attention during the past decade, and several more involved forms of tutoring have been developed that involve the entire general education classroom. The first of these newly developed systems is classwide peer tutoring (CWPT), which was developed in the 1980s by Charles Greenwood and his coworkers (Greenwood, 1991; Mortweet, Utley, Walker, Dawson, Delquadri, Reddy, & Greenwood, 1999; Utley, Mortweet, & Greenwood, 1997). The program has been used successfully as an integration strategy for children with a range of disabilities in addition to high-risk students and students with learning disabilities, and it works very well in inclusive classrooms. Furthermore, CWPT may be used in many content subjects such as reading, vocabulary, spelling, and mathematics, and this versatility suggests that CWPT should be considered as one strategy for every inclusive classroom.

CWPT is reciprocal in nature, and unlike the peer tutoring options discussed previously, every student will serve as both tutor and tutee. Again, this makes this tutoring approach particularly appropriate in inclusive classes. During the CWPT sessions, all students are paired with a partner, and each student pair is assigned to one of two competing teams. One student, serving initially as the tutor, will use preselected materials and call out problems to the tutee. Halfway through each tutoring session—after approximately ten minutes—the teacher signals the students to change roles; the tutors then become tutees and vice versa.

The tutees earn points for their team by correctly responding to specific tasks when presented to them by the tutor (Utley et al., 1997), and the team with the most points wins. The winning team can be

☞ **Teaching Tip 5.4**

CWPT Spelling Lesson

To begin the teaching session, one student is designated as the first tutor and is provided with a list of preselected spelling words for the tutee. The tutor then presents an instructional item orally by calling out the word for the tutee to write, and the tutee must respond by writing the word correctly. If the answer is correct, the tutor awards 2 points by noting the correct answer on an answer response sheet. The tutor then calls out the next word on the list and continues to call out words until ten minutes have passed.

If an answer is incorrect, the tutor conducts an error correction procedure, as follows. First the tutor would provide the correct response by spelling the word out loud and/or writing it down for the tutee. Next, the tutor would request that the tutee write the word correctly three times. Finally, the tutor would award 1 point to the tutee for writing the word correctly three times. If the tutee fails to provide the correct answer (three times), the tutor orally and visually provides the tutee the correct response, proceeds to the next item, and no points are awarded (Arreaga-Mayer, 1998).

After a ten-minute tutoring session, the teacher announces that the time is up, and the students reverse roles. A list of spelling words preselected for the new tutee is taken out, and the former tutee becomes the new tutor for the next ten minutes, following the same procedures as above. When twenty minutes have passed, at the end of the reciprocal tutoring session, the students report their total points to the teacher. The teacher then records the points on the "team chart." The total points are compared and both teams are applauded—the winning team for winning and the losing team for their effort.

determined daily or weekly and is based on each team's total points. Another strength of this program is that the tutor and tutee roles are highly structured to ensure that tutees receive questions or problems rapidly and in a consistent format. This results in increased time-on-task for the tutees and makes this strategy particularly effective as a differentiated instruction strategy for students with learning disabilities. Furthermore, all students are trained during this process to become effective tutors, and the structure of the tutoring sessions ensures consistency of instruction across pairs of students (Greenwood, 1991; Maheady et al., 1988; Mortweet, Utley, Walker, Dawson, Delquadri, Reddy, & Greenwood, 1999). A more detailed example of a CWPT spelling lesson is presented in Teaching Tip 5.4.

📖 REFLECTIVE EXERCISE: CONTEMPLATING CWPT

Establishing a CWPT system may seem to be quite a chore, but teachers who have established this system have indicated that after the initial work, they were quite relieved to be teaching in this fashion. Consider how you may undertake this type of tutoring system in an oral reading daily exercise. Initially, you would specify an appropriate oral reading level for each class member and select some reading comprehension passages. What would be the next step in implementing the CWPT system? Is this a strategy you could implement in your teaching situation?

The Teacher's Role in CWPT

Although CWPT gives the teacher the option to have all of the students in the general education classroom involved in tutoring at the same time, the teacher's role is still critical. Prior to initiating CWPT, the teacher organizes the content of the course material into daily and weekly lessons and then formats the materials to be used by the students. Instruction is planned individually, and each student is assigned spelling, reading, math, or language arts work at his or her instructional level. Needless to say, this may take some time because many of the students will have different instructional needs, but this organization of the curricula content also allows the teacher to specifically differentiate the instruction based on the needs and learning styles of the particular learners.

Once the material is organized, training for the tutoring occurs simultaneously for all tutor-tutee pairs involving the entire class at the same time (Arreaga-Mayer, 1998; Greenwood, 1991; Maheady et al., 1988; Mortweet, Utley, Walker, Dawson, Delquadri, Reddy, & Greenwood, 1999), and this is a major advantage of this method in general education classrooms. This procedure will free the teacher to supervise and monitor all students' responses during the tutoring sessions.

Students should be trained in the use of CWPT through modeling and practice from the teacher, as described previously for Level 3 tutoring tasks. The teacher starts by explaining how the "game" (i.e., the tutoring) works, including a discussion of winning teams, points, and tutoring. Students are introduced to both worksheets and scoring sheets for various types of activities. Emphasis should be placed on the concept of good sportsmanship during the tutoring sessions. The teacher then demonstrates by having a student perform the schoolwork as the tutee/student while the teacher acts as the tutor. The awarding of points is demonstrated, as is the appropriate error correction procedure. The teacher then selects two additional students to model tutoring procedures in front of the class while the other students watch, and the teacher

provides feedback. After a few demonstrations, the teacher has all students
practice the tutoring procedure (Arreaga-
Mayer, 1998), and actual CWPT may
begin the next day.

> Instruction is planned individu-
> ally, and each student is as-
> signed spelling, reading, math,
> or language arts work at his or
> her instructional level.

After the training phase, during the
actual CWPT procedure, the teacher's
role is that of monitoring the tutoring sessions. The teacher will evaluate the qual-
ity of tutoring, correcting tutoring procedures, as necessary, and may
award bonus points to tutors for demonstrating correct teaching behaviors. In this monitoring role (rather than the traditional lecture or discussion leader role), the teacher is free to respond immediately as students
request assistance. Again, this results in increased instructional time
attention provided for students with learning disabilities in general education classes because the teacher can respond more freely, and one half
of the students in the class are also providing instruction. Furthermore,
because of this careful monitoring on the part of the teacher, CWPT is a
system that engages students with the subject matter at higher levels.
Students doing CWPT usually spend 75 to 95% of the session engaged in
the learning task, and that on-task time is quite high for students with
learning disabilities in any educational endeavor (Utley et al., 1997).

CWPT has been proven beneficial in a variety of subject areas for
both elementary and high school levels. For example, at the elementary
level, CWPT is designed to supplement traditional instruction and to replace seatwork, lecture, and oral reading group activities. At the secondary level, CWPT is often focused on practice, skill building, and review
of subject matter. Building- and system-level CWPT procedures also are
available for supporting the implementation of this tutoring system
schoolwide (Mortweet, Utley, Walker, Dawson, Delquadri, Reddy, &
Greenwood, 1999; Utley et al., 1997).

Advantages of CWPT

A number of advantages of CWPT make this system particularly
effective in inclusive general education classrooms. First, CWPT can be
used in conjunction with teacher-made instructional materials or with
commercial curriculum materials, and thus one does not have to "purchase" specific materials to use CWPT. Next, CWPT enlists extensive
help and influence of the classroom peer group in the teaching process,
and depending on the age of the students involved, this can be a powerful instructional method. Students can and often do learn a great deal
from each other, and teachers in today's classrooms must learn to take
advantage of the power of students learning from other students
through tutoring.

Next, the reward system of individual students in CWPT depends not just on their own performance but also on the performance of other members on the team. This offers the advantage of strengthening the social interaction possibilities for students with learning disabilities.

> The teacher will evaluate the quality of tutoring, correcting tutoring procedures, as necessary, and may award bonus points to tutors for demonstrating correct teaching behaviors.

Changing the tutor-tutee pairs weekly and changing the roles within daily sessions keep the students motivated and provide for a variety of social interactions that may not occur in more traditionally taught classrooms. Each student is also provided the opportunity to learn teaching skills needed in the teacher's role (Mortweet, Utley, Walker, Dawson, Delquadri, Reddy, & Greenwood, 1999; Utley et al., 1997).

Several studies demonstrate the positive outcomes for students with learning disabilities and other disabilities using CWPT (Greenwood, 1991; Greenwood, Delquadri, & Hall, 1989; Maheady et al., 1988; Mortweet, Utley, Walker, Dawson, Delquadri, Reddy, & Greenwood, 1999; Utley et al., 1997). For example, Maheady et al. (1988) reported on a classwide peer tutoring system in a secondary resource room program for students with mild disabilities. Twenty students, fourteen males and six females, were enrolled in two separate sections of a secondary resource program for students with mild disabilities (i.e., learning disabilities, behavior disorders, or mild mental retardation). The students attended the resource room for approximately four periods a day for forty-five minutes each period and received instruction in reading,

> Students doing CWPT usually spend 75 to 95% of the session engaged in the learning task, and that on-task time is quite high for students with learning disabilities in any educational endeavor.

math, social studies, and daily living skills. The effectiveness of CWPT on students' weekly social studies quiz performance was assessed using a withdrawal of treatment design across two settings—teacher-led instruction and CWPT. To establish a baseline, the investigators began by having the teacher instruct her class using traditional teaching routines. This involved teacher-led lecture and discussion, occasional media presentations, assigned independent seatwork, and so on. Classwide peer tutoring was introduced into each classroom during the fourth week of the study. New classroom material continued to be introduced via two days of teacher lecture/discussion followed by assigned seatwork and homework during this phase. In addition, CWPT was implemented for thirty minutes per day for two days a week. The dependent variable was the percentage of correct answers on weekly social studies quizzes. The results indicated that the CWPT program significantly improved the weekly social studies test performance of students with mild disabilities. Close examination of the data revealed that almost all subjects were earning above 90% on the quizzes during CWPT instruction, and few participants received failing grades.

Mortweet, Utley, Walker, Dawson, Delquadri, Reddy, and Greenwood (1999) investigated the academic effects of CWPT for students with mild disabilities and their typical peers in two inclusive classroom settings. Twenty-five students without diagnosed disabilities and two students with mild mental retardation were enrolled in each classroom. Data were collected on the two students with

> CWPT can be used in conjunction with teacher-made instructional materials or with commercial curriculum materials, and thus one does not have to "purchase" specific materials to use CWPT.

mild mental retardation and two typical peers from each classroom. The four students with mild mental retardation were included in the general education classrooms for spelling, a social activity period, and a lunch period in accordance with their individualized education programs. A withdrawal of treatment design was employed to compare the effects of teacher-led instruction with CWPT on spelling test performance. Each target student's rate of academic engagement was observed once during each teacher-led instruction and CWPT condition. Spelling instruction in both classrooms consisted of twenty minutes of teacher-specified lessons using a grade-level spelling book. During the teacher-led instruction in one classroom, the teacher used small groups of two to three students and individual seat assignments for spelling instruction. The teacher in the other classroom mainly used whole-class lectures and picture flash cards of the spelling words for spelling lessons during the teacher-led instruction phase. The CWPT phase in each class employed Greenwood's (1991) model for CWPT. Dependant measures included performance on weekly spelling tests and direct observations of academic engagement. The results of this study demonstrated that CWPT was more effective than teacher-led instruction for both increasing spelling accuracy and increasing levels of on-task time for students with disabilities.

> Changing the tutor-tutee pairs weekly and changing the roles within daily sessions keep the students motivated and provide for a variety of social interactions that may not occur in more traditionally taught classrooms.

The studies to date have demonstrated the effectiveness of CWPT in the areas of reading, spelling, vocabulary, and math (Lazerson et al., 1988; Maheady et al., 1988; Mortweet, Utley, Walker, Dawson, Delquadri, Reddy, & Greenwood, 1999). Several used single-subject and experimental control group designs that included students with learning disabilities, behavior disorders, or mild mental retardation, and all of these studies have shown positive outcomes. Furthermore, CWPT has been reported to be effective with secondary students with mild disabilities and students with disabilities in inclusive settings (Maheady et al., 1988; Mortweet, Utley, Walker, Dawson, Delquadri, Reddy, & Greenwood, 1999). Clearly, this tutoring strategy should be employed in many general education classes for students with learning disabilities.

PEER-ASSISTED LEARNING STRATEGIES (PALS)

Peer-assisted learning strategies (PALS) is another highly structured peer tutoring system, which was developed in the early 1990s to provide general education teachers an effective, feasible, and acceptable intervention for the entire class (Fuchs et al., 2001; Fulk & King, 2001; Utley et al., 1997). Fuchs, Fuchs, Hamlett, Phillips, and Bentz (1995) observed that general education teachers made less adaptation in their classroom instructions to address the special needs of students with learning disabilities. This was the case even after teachers had been provided frequent information on the progress or lack of progress of individual students. To address the need for general educators to provide differentiated instruction in the inclusive classes, these authors recommended that general educators use curriculum-based measurement within the context of classwide peer tutoring structures to differentiate class instruction for students with learning disabilities (Utley et al., 1997). Curriculum-based measurement involves frequent measures of student performance embedded within the daily instructional tasks. Thus, in doing curriculum-based measurement, students typically complete work for a grade each day and chart that performance to generate a highly sensitive indicator of their daily learning progress.

PALS is built around a classwide tutoring concept, but it includes a number of different instructional approaches that are linked to computerized curriculum-based measurement. For example, math in PALS provides teachers with group and individual progress reports on a student's learning of specific math skills using classwide curriculum-based measurement (Fuchs et al., 2001). This enables the teacher to provide instruction to the group as well as address the needs of specific students. A PALS tutoring session is described in Teaching Tip 5.5.

Research on the effectiveness of PALS provides convincing support for its superiority compared to conventional general education instruction in reading and math (Fuchs et al., 2001; Fulk & King, 2001; Mathes, Fuchs, Fuchs, & Henley, 1994; Utley et al., 1997). The results of these studies indicated that all students with and without learning disabilities made measurably greater progress on test scores in the same amount of

☛ **Teaching Tip 5.5**

A PALS Tutoring Lesson

The three parts to PALS are *partner reading, paragraph shrinking,* and *prediction relay.*

In a reading lesson using PALS, each student reads aloud for ten minutes. The higher performing student reads the lesson first. The lower performing student rereads the same material. Whenever a reading error occurs, the tutor says, "Stop. You missed that word. Can you figure it out?" The reader either figures out the word within four seconds or the tutor says the word. Then the reader says the word. Then the tutor says, "Good job. Read the sentence again." Students earn 1 point for each correctly read sentence (if a word-reading correction is required, 1 point is awarded after the sentence is read correctly) and 10 points for the retell. After both students read, the lower performing student retells for two minutes the sequence of what occurred in the text (Fuchs, Fuchs, & Kazdan, 1999).

In paragraph shrinking (i.e., paragraph summarization), the tutors guide the identification of the main idea by asking readers to identify who or what the paragraph is mainly about and the most important thing about the who or what. The reader is required to put these two pieces of information together in ten or fewer words. When the tutor determines that a paragraph summary error has occurred, he or she says, "That's not quite right. Skim the paragraph and try again." The reader skims the paragraph and tries to answer the missed question. The tutor decides whether to give points or give the answer. For each summary, students earn 1 point for correctly identifying the who or what, 1 point for correctly stating the most important thing, and 1 point for using ten or fewer words. Students continue to monitor and correct reading errors, but points are no longer awarded on a sentence-by-sentence basis. After five minutes, the students switch roles (Fuchs et al., 1999).

In prediction relay, the reader makes a prediction about what will be learned on the next half page. The reader reads the half page aloud while the tutor identifies and corrects reading errors, (dis)confirms the prediction, and summarizes the main idea of the half page. When the tutor judges that a prediction is not realistic, he or she says, "I don't agree. Think of a better prediction." Otherwise, the word reading and paragraph summary correction procedures are used. The student receives 1 point for each viable prediction, 1 point for reading each half page, 1 point for accurately (dis)confirming each prediction, and 1 point for each component (i.e., the who or what and what mainly happened in 10 or fewer words) of each summary. After five minutes, the students switch roles (Fuchs et al., 1999).

> Research on the effectiveness of PALS provides convincing support for its superiority compared to conventional general education instruction in reading and math.

time. Teachers and students both reported high levels of satisfaction with PALS instruction (Fuchs et al., 2001; Mathes et al., 1994; Utley et al., 1997).

CONCLUSION

Regardless of the tutoring approach one selects, peer tutoring is one of the most effective tactics available to assist students with learning disabilities in the differentiated classroom. Using these methods, teachers can differentiate instruction and address the instructional needs of many students, including students with disabilities in the general education class. Research has been strongly supportive of each of the peer tutoring methodologies described above; both tutors and tutees learn more and are engaged more in tutoring situations than in traditional classroom instruction.

What's Next?

This chapter described several peer tutoring models that can enable the general education teacher to implement some type of peer tutoring system. Such a system will generally save the teacher time in the class and can therefore greatly enhance the opportunities for implementing various differentiated instructional strategies. Also, peer tutoring changes the process of learning and tends to emphasize relationships between students, which grow as a result of the tutoring process. In the next chapter, the focus will be placed on the final of the three major elements of differentiated instruction, differentiation of evaluation of the products produced by the students.

6

Supporting Students Through Performance Monitoring

Strategies Included in This Chapter:

✔ Curriculum-Based Assessment

✔ Precision Teaching

✔ Performance Assessment

✔ Portfolio Assessment

THE IMPORTANCE OF MONITORING STUDENT PERFORMANCE

As noted in previous chapters, students with learning disabilities in the general education classroom will require much more support for their learning efforts than do other children, and one of the most effective supports teachers can offer is an effective system for monitoring student performance (Fuchs et al., 2000; Gregory & Chapman, 2002, pp. 37-56; Jones, 2001a; Mathes, Fuchs, Roberts, & Fuchs, 1998). Thus, in the differentiated classroom, teachers will typically initiate a performance-monitoring system to support students academically, and this may include performance assessment measures, portfolios, or curriculum-based assessment procedures. This monitoring of daily performance will frequently result in charts of performance data on specific objectives from the child's individualized education program. Most students with learning disabilities respond quite favorably to seeing their academic progress charted, and this can become, for many students with learning disabilities, a very effective motivational tool. Many students will strive to post a "better" score today than yesterday; in fact, this phenomenon is frequently commented on when I require a daily databased performance chart as a class project in my graduate special education methods class.

Within the past twenty-five years, a number of tactics have been developed for portraying a student's progress over time in charted form, and to offer the most effective supports for students with learning disabilities, teachers must delineate a system of charting progress for most students with learning disabilities in the inclusive class. Because the behavioral model of learning—which has been so influential in special education—emphasized accurate measurement, many performance-monitoring systems are founded on it, and teachers who are moving toward a more differentiated class frequently adopt this innovation.

Still, the concentration on frequent assessment and monitoring of student performance on curricular skills is a relatively new direction (Fuchs & Deno, 1994; Fuchs, Fuchs, Hamlett, Phillips, & Bentz, 1994; Jones, 2001b; Wesson, 1991) and has not yet been totally accepted by teachers in the field. Whereas traditional assessment often emphasized measurement of cognitive ability deficits (e.g., auditory perception, visual memory, or other disabilities that may hamper learning) or occasional measures of academic performance on a limited number of test questions, the newer emphasis involved direct assessment of academic skills within the curriculum. Thus, researchers in the field use the terms *curriculum-based assessment* or *curriculum-based measurement* (Jones, 2001b).

A commonplace example will serve to illustrate the importance of this concept. When a student is assessed for special education, numerous tests are given that measure skills and abilities that are not included in the school curriculum—tests such as tests of intelligence, memory, attention skills, and/or visual/auditory perception ability. These "ability" areas are not included in the school curriculum because changing these specific abilities is not the purpose of instruction. Although we traditionally tested students with learning disabilities in these areas to identify the root problems a child with a learning disability may experience, we generally did not attempt to teach these specific skills. Rather, these abilities were believed to enhance or limit the capacity of a child to master the academic skills in math, reading, and/or language arts and thus were worthy of measurement.

Of course, assessment of these noncurriculum abilities has been challenged repeatedly over the years (Linn, 1986; Marston, Tindal, & Deno, 1984). For example, some theorists have argued that the tests used to measure innate ability are highly suspect on technical grounds, and others have suggested that assessment should focus on skills that can be

Some kids daydream.

taught (Linn, 1986). However, scholars agree that through repeatedly measuring a child's progress on a particular set of academic skills, rather than on these noncurricular abilities, we obtain information that is much more useful for planning the next instructional tasks for that child (Fuchs et al., 2000; Jones, 2001a; Mathes et al., 1998; White, 1986). For these reasons, assessment based directly on the skills in the child's curriculum, measured on a repeated and frequent basis, seems to be the option of choice for students with learning disabilities.

Scholars disagree on the frequency with which a child's behavior should be assessed in curriculum-based assessment models. For example, some theorists argue that a teacher-made assessment administered weekly may be sufficient (Peterson, Heistad, Peterson, & Reynolds, 1985), whereas others feel that student progress should be assessed every day (White, 1986). Despite these differences of opinion, the components of curriculum-based assessment are fairly widely accepted. These include the following:

1. That assessment for educational planning should be based only on the skills listed in the child's curriculum

2. That assessment should be repeated regularly and frequently throughout the year

3. That these repeated assessments should be used as the basis for educational decision making for the child with a learning disability

The last factor has proven to be a strong advantage in favor of curriculum-based assessment. As one example, most adults today can recall having a "trial test" on spelling words every Wednesday in elementary school, and that trial test was an attempt to prepare us for the "final test" on the same words on Friday. This is a good instructional technique because it allows the students to note their areas of deficiency on Wednesday, well in advance of the final, graded assessment on Friday. Also, on Thursday, the most effective elementary teachers would plan a spelling lesson that included an emphasis on the difficult words that were identified on the Wednesday test. In this example, educational activities were planned based on recent data concerning the actual academic performance of the students. When teachers extend this example to the logical conclusion, they may find that they are grading daily homework or class work on the spelling words and not conducting a final test on Friday at all! Thus, rather than generating a grade on one—relatively artificial—test of performance on Friday, the student's daily performance on the spelling exercises would serve as the basis for the spelling grade.

> Scholars agree that through repeatedly measuring a child's progress on a particular set of academic skills, rather than on noncurricular abilities, we obtain information that is much more useful for planning the next instructional tasks for that child.

Another example may be helpful. Imagine a teacher in the third-grade basic skills class who introduces two-digit multiplication on a Monday. After teaching for two weeks through examples on the dry-erase board, seatwork, and homework, she tests her students on the second Friday. To her surprise, she determines that half her class has not mastered this skill. Furthermore (although she may not realize it), several members of the class had mastered that new skill by the second day of the two-week lesson and did not really need to spend any additional time on that skill. Thus, their participation over the past two weeks has been wasted time. Clearly, this is not effective instruction for many students in that class.

Suppose, however, that the same teacher had used the daily worksheets as a continuing assessment and required that each student chart his or her performance after each day's lesson. After only one or two days, she would have discovered that some students had already mastered this skill, whereas other students whose daily work indicated problems with comprehension of this task would then be instructed on a one-on-one basis until they mastered the work. Obviously, repeated assessment, even when it is as informal as worksheets done in class, can be a very effective tool for instructional planning in the differentiated class. Furthermore, the more frequent the assessment (a daily basis assessment seems to be the general consensus), the more responsive the instruction can be. Finally, if the assessment data are summarized in some readily interpretable form, such as a chart of performance, this information is even more useful. Imagine the teacher in the example above having to look through all of the worksheets for each child to determine that child's progress, and compare that with the teacher looking at a simple chart of daily performance for each student; the latter summary of the data saves a great deal of time.

Theorists in curriculum-based assessment generally do not accept a distinction between "assessment" on one hand and "instruction" on the other. In fact, by basing instructional decisions on repeated measures of academic work, the traditional separation between "testing" and "teaching" becomes blurred. Furthermore, with comprehensive curriculum-based assessment data, it is possible to envision a day when more traditional assessments of innate abilities or unit tests of academic comprehension become obsolete (Fuchs et al., 2000; Jones, 2001b; Peterson et al., 1985).

Although that possibility has not yet been realized, this concept of basing instructional decisions on repeated measures of academic skills is the cornerstone of curriculum-based assessment. This concept represents one of the most powerful instructional strategies for students with learning disabilities, as well as for many other students in the differentiated class. The concept was based on several earlier research emphases, which are presented below. These include *criterion-referenced testing, precision teaching,* and *direct instruction,* and understanding these strategies will assist each teacher in preparing his or her curriculum-based assessment program for the inclusive class.

> Obviously, repeated assessment, even when it is as informal as worksheets done in class, can be a very effective tool for instructional planning in the differentiated class.

CRITERION-REFERENCED TESTING

Criterion-referenced testing (CRT) served as one basis for the development of curriculum-based assessment (Jones, 2001b). Most assessments compare a student's performance with the performance of a group of students on whom the assessment was normed. The scores and information for that norm group are usually published in the test's manual, and that group serves as the basis to generate the commonly accepted scores on the test—the grade-equivalent or norm-based scores. In contrast to this "norm group" comparison score, the purpose of the criterion-referenced test is to compare a student's performance to a specific set of

☞ **Teaching Tip 6.1**

Criterion-Referenced Test in Whole-Number Addition

1.	5	7	4	2	8	
	+2	+2	+4	+6	+2	Percentage Score _____

2.	6	3	8	2	9	
	+8	+9	+4	+4	+2	Percentage Score _____ .

3.	35	47	54	25	83	
	+42	+32	+24	+13	+22	Percentage Score _____

4.	27	27	37	28	69	
	+46	+25	+34	+13	+22	Percentage Score _____

5.	64	87	98	79	78	
	+36	+35	+24	+14	+22	Percentage Score _____

6.	73	87	98	76	81	
	+36	+35	+21	+13	+22	Percentage Score _____

academic skills that are appropriate for the student's age and grade level (Monda-Amoya & Reed, 1993). Thus, a criterion-referenced test is an assessment that lists sequenced behavioral skills in a particular area and compares a student's performance to the optimal performance on the listed objectives. For example, consider the sequenced skills involved in whole-number addition. A test including the specific types of problems associated with each individual skill in this area would involve some problems such as those presented in Teaching Tip 6.1.

With a criterion-referenced assessment along these lines in hand, it is relatively easy to determine the specific skills on which a student with a learning disability has problems. If a student with a learning disability completed the first two rows of math problems at 80 or 100 percent accuracy and then achieved only 20 percent accuracy on the third row, the teacher could be fairly certain that the student was having a difficulty

Teaching Tip 6.2

Objectives for the Whole-Number Addition Problems on This CRT

1. When presented with a series of five whole-number single-digit addition problems involving math facts that sum to less than 10, the student will complete the problems with 100% accuracy.

2. When presented with a series of five whole-number single-digit addition problems involving math facts that sum to 10 or more, with regrouping in the 1s place, the student will complete the problems with 100% accuracy.

3. When presented with a series of five whole-number double-digit addition problems involving no regrouping, the student will complete the problems with 100% accuracy.

4. When presented with a series of five whole-number double-digit addition problems involving regrouping in the 1s place, the student will complete the problems with 100% accuracy.

5. When presented with a series of five whole-number double-digit addition problems involving regrouping in the 1s place and the 10s place, the student will complete the problems with 100% accuracy.

6. When presented with a series of five whole-number double-digit addition problems involving regrouping in the 1s place, the 10s place, or both, the student will complete the problems with 100% accuracy.

understanding the concept of regrouping or place value because that is the difference between the problems completed successfully and those that were not completed successfully. In other words, the student would need specific work on place value and regrouping.

The sequenced objectives associated with each type of problem on a CRT are typically printed in the test manual. For informal CRTs that are developed by the teacher, objectives could be written and attached to the individualized education program for the student. A list of objectives for the whole-number addition CRT are presented in Teaching Tip 6.2.

Of course, use of a CRT on one occasion during the school year does not constitute curriculum-based assessment. Clearly, although CRT assessment is preferable to assessment of intelligence or other ability deficits discussed previously, the last two components of curriculum-based assessment from the list above cannot be addressed if the CRT is administered only once during a school year. Curriculum-based

The sequenced objectives associated with each type of problems on a CRT are typically printed in the test manual.

assessment requires frequently repeated CRTs to allow for instructional decisions based directly on student performance (Jones, 2001b), and this strategy is one of the most powerful teaching strategies that can be used for students with learning disabilities.

REFLECTIVE EXERCISE: WHERE CAN YOU DO CURRICULUM-BASED ASSESSMENT?

If you wished to find a motivating tool for a student with a learning disability, curriculum-based assessment (CBA) may be the tool you are looking for. Are there students in your class for whom you cannot seem to find an effective motivation? You may wish to initiate a CBA project and offer the entire class some reinforcement on days when the individual student's performance increases in comparison with the day before. Would this be an option in your class?

PRECISION TEACHING

Precision teaching is a method for closely monitoring the academic performance of students that originated in the "behavioral school" of psychology (Lindsley, 1971; Vail & Huntington, 1993; Wesson, 1991; White, 1986). Of course, behavioral psychology emphasized readily observable behaviors, measured precisely, and antecedents or consequences that tended to increase or decrease these behaviors. When applying these behavioral principles to education, Lindsley (1971) enumerated five principles as having a direct bearing on educational success. Each of these principles, presented in Teaching Tip 6.3, relates directly to monitoring the individual performance of students on learning tasks, and for this reason, precision teaching provided one cornerstone for the current movement toward curriculum-based assessment.

Given the obvious emphasis on monitoring individual achievement in these principles, Lindsley (1971) developed a focus on charting specific behaviors of a student. First, the behavior was pinpointed by stating an appropriate behavioral objective. Behavioral objectives traditionally stipulated three things: the task the student would perform, the conditions under which the student would perform the task, and the criteria used to evaluate the performance.

An example of a behavioral objective would be as follows:

☞ **Teaching Tip 6.3**

Five Principles of Precision Teaching

1. *The learner knows best.* This principle suggests that if the child is progressing, the teaching method is appropriate, whereas if the child is not progressing, some other procedure must be tried. In short, only the learner's actual progress is a valid measure of success or failure of a particular instructional method.

2. *Focus on directly observable behavior.* Lindsley (1971) demanded that teachers focus on behavior that is observable to glean a clear, unambiguous picture of progress.

3. *Frequency is the measure of behavior.* Because of the dissatisfactions with tabulation of correct responses as a measure of success, the focus in precision teaching is frequency or rate of the response (how many correct responses per minute the child demonstrates).

4. *Use of a standard chart for measuring success.* Charting has numerous advantages over other methods of measuring success, and charts of pupil progress are a *must* for the precision teacher.

5. *Description of environmental conditions.* A teacher must understand the effect of the environment on the child's behavior and be able to construct the appropriate antecedent and consequent conditions that shape behavior. Consequently, knowing what the child can do (prerequisite behaviors) facilitates the decision making for the present instructional sequence. For a more complete description of these five principles, see Lindsley (1971) and White (1986).

> When presented with twenty double-digit addition problems that do not involve regrouping, the student will complete the problems with 90% accuracy.

This is a relatively standard behavioral objective, and the three components are evident. With this type of objective in hand, the teacher's job becomes relatively easy. The student must be instructed in this skill and repeatedly assessed until he or she meets the criteria stipulated in the objective. Performance may be charted daily on a simple graph such as that presented in Teaching Tip 6.4, and for most students with learning disabilities, the chart itself will serve as a motivator and reinforcer. Furthermore, when the student reaches mastery for three consecutive days, he or she is ready to move on to the next skill in the academic sequence—in this case, double-digit addition with regrouping.

However, Lindsley and his colleagues quickly realized that the problems of some students were not related to their *accuracy* but rather to their *speed* in completing problems in class. Needless to say, this is true of many students with learning disabilities, making the precision teaching

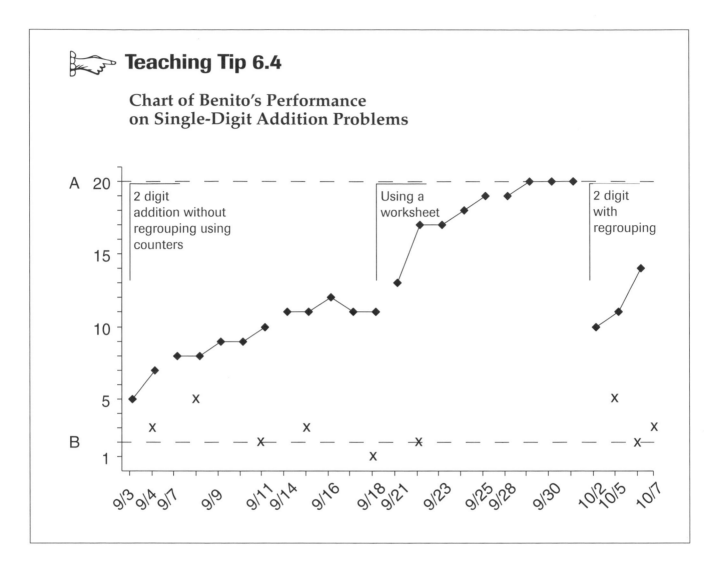

Teaching Tip 6.4

Chart of Benito's Performance on Single-Digit Addition Problems

innovation a critical instructional option for these students. Clearly, for some students with learning disabilities, the problem is to get them to work both correctly and quickly, and this is the one of the few instructional methods to address that critical concern. For this reason, Lindsley (1971) introduced the idea of behavioral objectives that specify a certain rate (i.e., speed) of behavior as follows:

> When presented with a page of double-digit addition problems that do not require regrouping, the student will successfully complete an average of twenty problems during each two-minute period.

With this type of objective in hand, students and teachers were prepared to concentrate their focus on the speed of the work as well as the accuracy.

A Sample of Precision Teaching

Based on the principles listed above and this "rate-based perfor-mance" idea, Lindsley (1971) developed the concept of precision teach-ing. Teaching Tip 6.4 presents a behavioral chart of Benito's performance on the objective above. The dots represent correct problems, and the *x*s indicate the number of errors for each day. For exam-ple, Benito answered seventeen problems correctly and had two errors on Tuesday, September 22. You will also note a dashed line on the "20" line. This represents the "aim line," or the goal expressed in the objective. For most students with learning disabilities, reaching the aim line for three days becomes a very rewarding experi-ence. The dashed line on the "2" line is called the "record floor." This indicates the length of the timed exercise, as described in the objective. In addition to the terms *record floor* and *aim line,* precision teaching, as ini-tially recommended, involved the use of many additional terms—that is, a language of precision in teaching—as well as a particular type of chart for charting of performance data. Although most teachers have left these nuances behind, the concept of data charted on a daily basis as the deci-sion-making tool was one cornerstone of precision teaching that has endured and forms one basis for the current initiatives in curriculum-based performance monitoring.

> For some students with learning disabilities, the problem is to get them to work both correctly and quickly, and this is the one of the few instructional methods to address that critical concern.

In reviewing the chart, you will notice that during the week of Sep-tember 14 through September 18, Benito did not continue to make prog-ress. Whenever three days of "flat data" are recorded, the teacher and the student must make some type of change because the data have demon-strated that the instructional exercises are not showing any results. This type of decision making is highly sensitive to the instructional needs of the student with learning disabilities, and this precision in instructional decision making was one goal of precision teaching theorists.

Notice the "phase change" lines at the top of the chart. These indicate that instruction was adjusted, either because the warm-up activities were not effective or because Benito reached the aim. For example, dur-ing the week of September 14 through 18, the instructional activity involved the use of counters to complete the addition problems. On each of these days, Benito spent five to ten minutes working a page of prob-lems using counters to represent each of the digits in the 1s column and each of the digits in the 10s column. After a warm-up session, Benito would indicate that he was ready for the timing. The teacher would hand Benito a worksheet of math problems and begin a two-minute timing. After the time period ended, Benito would use a self-check answer sheet to check his answers and count the number of correct answers.

> This type of decision making is highly sensitive to the instructional needs of the student with learning disabilities.

The chart shows that, on September 18, the teacher and Benito jointly decided that the warm-up activity was not helping Benito improve his work. Consequently, the phase change line on September 21 indicated that a new warm-up activity was in use: completion of problems on a worksheet without using counters. Apparently, this activity worked out well because Benito began to show progress and reached aim for three days at the end of the next week. The next phase change line (October 5) indicates that Benito moved on to the next math skill in the sequence—double-digit addition with regrouping in the 1s place.

Initiation of a Precision Teaching Project

Many teachers have students with learning disabilities in their classes who never seem to complete the assigned work. For those students, a precision teaching performance-monitoring tactic may be exactly what is needed because this is one of the few instructional strategies that directly address the speed with which children with learning disabilities complete their work. When initiating a precision teaching instructional project, certain steps should be followed.

First, you will need to delineate a series of sequential behavioral objectives for the project. The objective should be stated as a "rate-based behavior" and specify a length of time or rate of behavior.

REFLECTIVE EXERCISE: DEVELOPING RATE-BASED OBJECTIVES

Teachers may wish to take the objectives in Teaching Tip 6.2 and make each a rate-based objective. All that the teachers need to add is the phrase "in a one-minute period" to the end of each objective. How could these objectives be turned into two-minute objectives, and does that change the number of required successes in the objective?

Second, you should discuss the objectives with the student with the learning disability and make every effort to get the student to "buy into" the objective. The relationship that the teacher has with the student will be critical at this point, and this effort to get the student to take responsibility for learning reflects the emphasis on personal responsibility for learning, as discussed in Chapter 2.

Next, teachers will need to establish a goal—called an aim line—for the student with the learning disability. Although precision teaching theorists have recommended different procedures for setting the aim, the simplest method is to have the student's performance timed for three days and then use that information for an educated "guess" at an appropriate aim. Note that the aim line should reflect a performance for each individual student, and aims for one student should not be automatically used for other students.

Finally, the teacher will want to select a three- to five-minute instructional warm-up activity directly related to the objectives. For example, flash cards may be good exercise for math facts. Likewise, "word window" exercises that reveal only one syllable of multisyllabic spelling words may be appropriate for a spelling or language arts exercise.

Note that, unlike many of the other differentiated instructional tactics described in this text, precision teaching is really somewhat eclectic in that no particular teaching method is recommended. The teacher is free to choose any instructional tactic as a warm-up activity that may work for the student with the learning disability. In this sense, precision teaching must be considered an instructional monitoring technique rather than a single instructional teaching strategy itself.

It is quite possible to develop a precision teaching monitoring system for almost any instructional strategy; even metacognitive techniques such as reciprocal teaching exercises could be structured to conclude with an objective comprehension test on each day for each student, and those data could be charted! This performance-monitoring aspect of precision teaching makes this strategy much more reactive to the individual needs of students with learning disabilities and gives the teacher the necessary information to make very frequent instructional decisions for students with learning disabilities in the inclusive class.

> A precision teaching performance monitoring tactic may be exactly what is needed because this is one of the few instructional strategies that directly address the speed with which children with learning disabilities complete their work.

Precision teaching performance monitoring may also be used for the entire inclusive class. In essence, using precision teaching typically involves using a worksheet and counting students' correct problems in a given amount of time. Students with and without learning disabilities in the general education class can be taught to do this work and subsequently to chart their own performance from day to day. Thus, inclusive teachers, working two teachers per class, may wish to use precision teaching with the entire group. However, even in the general education class, when a special education teacher is not present, precision teaching will assist in saving time for the teacher because students will, over time, take much more responsibility for their own work.

Another option is to do all of the timed work during the last fifteen minutes of the inclusive class period. For example, Benito may have the addition worksheet, a worksheet on identification of subjects and predicates, and a worksheet on punctuation. Other students would likewise have several timed worksheets to complete, and the length of their various timings would probably vary. After checking to see that each student had the correct worksheets, the teacher would start a bell-tone tape that rang a bell at one-minute intervals and merely leave it running. When Benito finishes a two-minute timing, he could use the next couple of minutes to check his work and put his score on the math chart. When the next bell rings, he would begin his language arts worksheet for a one-minute timing. Other students would be completing other worksheets specifically designated for the two-, four-, or ten-minute timed exercises.

Advantages of Precision Teaching

The advantages of this system over traditional group instruction are numerous. First, this instructional monitoring procedure makes instruction highly sensitive to the needs of students with learning disabilities, as shown in various research efforts (White, 1986). Specifically, some aspect of instruction for the student must change if three days' data are "flat" because "flat data" on a chart represent no progress. Teachers may change the warm-up activity, identify a particular prerequisite behavior the student did not have, or provide tangible reinforcement for correct responses above a certain level. The point is that something must change if the data reveal that the current instructional tactics are not working. Obviously, if the student attains aim for three consecutive days, he or she should move to the next skill in the sequence.

> Note that, unlike many of the other differentiated instructional tactics described in this text, precision teaching is really somewhat eclectic in that no particular teaching method is recommended.

Second, each student is instructed as an individual, as mandated by special education law. Furthermore, when using precision teaching, there is a demonstrated and direct relationship between the particular objectives on a student's individualized education program (IEP) and the daily work in class for each student with a learning disability. Surprisingly, such a relationship is not always apparent in much instruction in special education and/or inclusive classes. Also, this relationship between the objectives and the actual worksheets done in class can easily be communicated to parents and to the student with the learning disability by using the chart; that is, the chart serves to make the educational attainment very "real."

Third, when a student's progress is graphically portrayed, the students tend to "own" more responsibility for achieving the goals set forth in their educational program. Achieving aim—in and of itself—becomes reinforcing for most students with learning disabilities. Fourth, instructional decisions may be made on a daily basis, which minimizes the wasted time associated with two- or three-week unit tests. Finally, communication with other teachers is facilitated by showing progress using the data charts. In fact, charted data can become one of the most effective communication mechanisms for teacher-to-teacher communication. With these advantages in mind, application of precision teaching will increase for students with learning disabilities. Precision teacher materials are currently available from a company called Sopris West in Longmont, Colorado (these are referred to as their "Basic Skills" curriculum).

> When using precision teaching, there is a demonstrated and direct relationship between the particular objectives on a student's individualized education program (IEP) and the daily work in class for each student with a learning disability.

DIRECT INSTRUCTION

Direct instruction is a set of behaviorally oriented instructional procedures that involve both the concept of frequent academic performance monitoring and the principles of effective instruction. Practically speaking, the term *direct instruction* has at least two meanings, depending on the theorists or practitioner using it. Initially, the term meant the application of a number of specific teaching behaviors that tended to lead to higher student achievement among all students. These behaviors, presented in Teaching Tip 6.5, were specified in the body of research that has become identified as the effective teaching research. These teaching behaviors have received overwhelming research support during the past thirty years, and all teachers should exemplify these instructional behaviors in dealing with students with and without learning disabilities (Baumann, 1984, 1986).

Gersten, Woodward, and Darch (1986) used this comprehensive definition in a discussion of the effectiveness of direct instruction, which included such components as curriculum design, classroom management, and teacher preparation. These and other theorists have recommended application of direct instruction to students with learning disabilities (Wilson & Sindelar, 1991), and when researchers say "direct instruction," this set of effective teaching behaviors is probably the concept to which they are referring.

However, the effective teaching behaviors have been the basis for the development of certain commercially available curriculum materials over the years, and for many practitioners, the term *direct instruction* has taken on this more limited definition—that is, the use of curriculum materials that embody the effective teaching behaviors. Thus, when

☞ Teaching Tip 6.5

Ten Effective Teaching Behaviors to Improve Your Teaching!

1. *Lead the instruction.* Teachers should directly lead the instruction of pupils in small-group activities. Research has consistently supported teacher-led instruction as the most effective type of instruction.

2. *Visually monitor student behaviors.* Teachers should visually monitor each student's attention to task. When students are attending to the educational task, they will master the material much more quickly and will learn more.

3. *Conduct orientation to the lesson.* The teacher should orient the students to the lesson as a first step in teaching each lesson. Teachers should let students know clearly what is expected of them for a particular lesson, relate that expectation to previous lessons, and highlight what students should be able to do after they learn the material.

4. *Model the lesson tasks.* In conducting the lesson, the teacher should frequently model the new task to be learned and note problem areas in performing each new task.

5. *Monitor the instructional outcomes on specific objectives.* Teachers should monitor the academic performance for each student during the lesson and on a daily basis throughout a series of lessons. This is typically done with some type of chart of academic performance.

6. *Ask questions.* Frequently asked questions during the lesson can help students focus on the task more effectively. Teachers should wait an appropriate time after asking a question (see the discussion of wait time in an earlier chapter) and require several students to answer each question. Each student response can be considered a "product" that the student has to produce to move through the learning.

7. *Require regular products from the students.* When students are required to produce work, they learn more, and effective teachers require regular products from the students (projects, worksheets, groupwork, homework, etc.).

8. *Provide constant and timely feedback to students.* Students learn much more from corrected errors than from work done correctly. Thus, teachers should regularly respond to students' work, with detailed written or verbal feedback. This would include answering questions in class, addressing errors on homework, and correcting students' class work in a timely fashion.

9. *Ensure that each student has reached a mastery level.* Because much learning is cumulative and built on prerequisite skills (one learns the noun and verb as the first parts of speech and, subsequently, the adjective, adverb, etc.), students must reach a certain mastery on the early skills to even undertake work on subsequent skills. Most teachers look for mastery levels of 85 to 95% since mastery levels in this range are required prior to moving on to subsequent material.

10. *Praise students frequently for successful work.* Students respond to positive praise quite favorably, and students with learning disabilities are praised much less than other students in the inclusive classroom. Thus, as long as the praise is valid (i.e., praise for work well done and not for some "imagined" success on the part of the student—indeed, this false praise will turn students off!), students with learning disabilities cannot be praised too much!

many teachers say, "direct instruction," they usually mean one of several commercially available instructional materials in reading, math, or language arts.

These materials typically include a teacher's instructional script and various structured lesson plans to be followed. Curriculum materials such as *Reading Mastery*, originally known as *DISTAR* (Engelmann & Carnine, 1972; Engelmann & Hanner, 1982) and *Corrective Reading: Comprehension Skills Comprehension* (Engelmann, Osborn, & Hanner, 1989), are direct instructional materials that were written to ensure that the teacher incorporates each of the effective teaching behaviors into the delivery of the lesson. These materials have been most closely associated with Scientific Research Associates of Chicago.

These materials have very specific "scripts" that the teacher is to read word for word when conducting the lesson on a particular topic. The scripts include alternative teacher responses for correct and incorrect answers that students may give. In fact, the lessons are so highly structured that some teachers have reported that using these scripts limited creativity in instruction. Nevertheless, research has strongly supported these curricula for students with learning disabilities. Teaching Tip 6.6 presents a sample scripted lesson.

Phases of Learning in Direct Instruction

The direct instruction literature posits four separate phases in the learning process, including lesson orientation, direct instruction, teacher-led practice, and independent practice.

Orientation to Learning. The instructional script states everything a teacher is supposed to say, beginning with an orientation to the lesson for the day. The scripts start with a few statements of dialogue that let the students know what the lesson is about. The task is stated clearly and briefly so that students can understand. Instructions to the students are kept simple and given at a brisk pace to keep the lesson moving along smoothly. Also, some discussion of the importance of mastering the objective is presented to help the students with learning disabilities understand the need to work hard and master the material. As mentioned in Chapter 2, students with learning disabilities need instruction that emphasizes personal involvement and personal responsibility, perhaps more so than students without disabilities, and this lesson orientation phase in direct instruction emphasizes personal involvement.

Direct Instruction Phase. Next comes the direct instruction phase, sometimes referred to as initial instruction. The scripted lesson would include a dialogue for the teacher to read that emphasized certain aspects of the instructional task (Baumann, 1984; Darch & Kameenui,

☞ Teaching Tip 6.6

A Sample Direct Instruction Script

Teacher: Listen. Here's a rule. Just because someone important in one area says something is good or bad in another area, you can't be sure it's true. (Repeat.)

Teacher: When someone important in one area says something is good or bad in another area, can you be sure it's true?

Student: No.

Teacher: No, just because someone important in one area says something is good or bad in another area, you can't be sure it's true.

Teacher: Ok, listen. Former President George Bush says that Dodge trucks are the best pick-up trucks available.

Teacher: What do you know about former President George Bush?

Student: He's an important person. He knows politics.

Teacher: In what area is he important?

Student: Politics around Washington.

Teacher: And what's this important person saying?

Student: That Dodge makes the best truck.

Teacher: So what is the area that he is talking about?

Student: Trucks.

Teacher: Since we're learning to judge what people say, can you be sure what a former president says about trucks is true?

Student: No.

Teacher: What can you say when someone important says something is good or bad?

Student: (Student should respond with something like,) You can't be sure it's true, if it's not his background or area of expertise.

Teacher: Listen, if I tell you that former President George Bush says that politics is a hard life, would you believe him?

Student: Yes. That's an area he knows about.

Correction procedure: If a child answers "No," ask, "What do you know about the important person?" And then review the rule above.)

Teacher: Yes, you can choose to believe that. Why?

(Accept the answer in varying form, provided that the following information is given: [1] he's a former president or politician, [2] former presidents know about politics, and [3] he's talking about something he knows about.)

1987). A sentence about the last lesson is sometimes included, and the teacher would be instructed to model the first step of the task. Students would be asked questions about the task. Several tasks may be completed jointly by the teacher and the student during this direct instruction phase, with the teacher assuming the major burden for the work.

The key distinction between direct instruction and other instruction programs is the explicit nature of instruction during this phase. The script instructs the teacher to present the examples, note problem areas, and model the task; each of these activities was identified as an effective teaching research referred to earlier, but unfortunately, many of these steps in learning are left out of traditional instructional techniques. In fact, proponents of direct instruction note that most instructional techniques, as exemplified by basal reading textbooks, are far from explicit in this phase (Kameenui, Carnine, Darch, & Stein, 1986).

Teacher-Directed Practice. After the direct instruction phase involving modeling with student participation, several practice tasks are given to the student. In these tasks, the teacher may verbally cue the students about the correct task procedure, but the responsibility for the task rests with the students. The scripted lesson includes explicit questions that the teacher is supposed to ask the students, and these questions exemplify the various possible trouble spots in task completion. Sometimes, this phase is referred to as the guided practice phase.

REFLECTIVE EXERCISE: EFFECTIVE TEACHING BEHAVIORS IN A DIRECT INSTRUCTION SCRIPT

Review the script in Teaching Tip 6.6 and identify specific examples of the ten effective teaching behaviors identified in Teaching Tip 6.5. Note, for example, the statements that exemplify the problem of identifying an invalid testimonial. This phase of instruction is presented as practice that gives the teacher the opportunity to repeatedly question the students about the task. The integration of these effective teaching behaviors into the scripted lessons makes this instructional approach highly effective in general education and special education classes. Do you think you would enjoy teaching from this type of lesson format?

In some scripts, there is a very clear delineation between the modeling, or direct instruction phase, and the teacher-directed practice phase, whereas in other materials the distinction is less clear. Still, at some point, the student assumes the major responsibility for task completion. During this phase, the teacher provides immediate feedback to the student to prevent continuation of incorrect problem solutions. This feedback is one of the cornerstones of direct instruction, as feedback of this nature was heavily emphasized in the effective learning research.

Independent Practice. After the student has demonstrated some competence in the teacher-directed practice phase, a series of problems are assigned for independent practice. At this point in the lesson, the script instructs the teacher to present various worksheets, projects, and assignments to the students. Generally, the tasks will require no more than half of the total lesson time. The student will work on these tasks alone and show the completed work to the teacher for checking. In some direct instruction curriculum materials, this phase of instruction may be done as homework, although most of the commercially available materials include some independent practice in the recommended class lesson time.

> In these tasks, the teacher may verbally cue the students about the correct task procedure, but the responsibility for the task rests with the students.

Because monitoring of student performance is one cornerstone of direct instruction, almost every commercially available direct instruction program includes procedures to monitor each student's success rate on a daily basis on these independent practice problems. You may also recall from Chapter 4 that the learning strategies curriculum described there included daily monitoring of student performance. In fact, almost all curriculum that has been developed subsequent to the development of direct instruction has incorporated daily performance monitoring as a result of the power of this technique.

Efficacy of Direct Instruction

Unlike research in certain other areas (e.g., the brain-compatible research), research on direct instruction has been ongoing for at least three decades. In fact, direct instruction is one of the most thoroughly researched instructional techniques available today, and the research has been quite positive. This instructional procedure works for students with learning disabilities, as it does for a variety of other groups of students. Specifically, direct instruction may be used to teach basic skills in reading, math, and language arts to very diverse groups of schoolchildren with a stunning success rate (Baumann, 1984, 1986; Darch & Gersten, 1986; Gersten et al., 1986; Polloway, Epstein, Polloway, Patton, & Ball, 1986; Rabren, Darch, & Eaves, 1999). Most of these studies compared a direct-instruction curriculum materials package to an instructional approach recommended in basal reading or math texts, and the results consistently favored the experimental group receiving direct instruction. Although there are studies that fail to document success in using direct instruction on students with learning disabilities (Kuder,

1990), other studies do document positive effects (Rabren et al., 1999), and these studies seem to be in the majority. Thus, it is accurate to say that the research on direct instruction is strongly positive for students with learning disabilities.

Implementation of Direct Instruction

Like many of the tactics that have been reviewed in this text, direct instruction may be implemented in the inclusive classroom with a little additional time and investment (Gersten et al., 1986). Teachers generally begin by using some of the commercially prepared materials. Teachers should ask their media person if these materials are available because many media centers did purchase many of these materials over the years. Next, teachers should carefully select the level of the materials to use, so that there is an appropriate match between learner needs and curriculum. Many of the direct instruction materials have pretests that may be used in this regard. These materials can be implemented in small reading groups, small math groups, or individually. Initially, teachers may wish to select one reading or math group and implement the lessons for a few days prior to beginning the lessons in other groups. The script is written in complete form, and every effort should be made to stay with the script because getting off the script breaks up the pacing of the lesson.

A major advantage of direct instruction is the fact that direct instruction works well in inclusive classes (Gersten et al., 1986). Because the direct instruction curricula suggest teacher-led, small-group instruction, many inclusive teachers who have formed reading or language arts study groups in the inclusive class may easily incorporate the direct instruction curriculum into their lower- or average-level reading groups.

> Although different scholars may disagree on specific instructional strategies as a "best practice," for students with learning disabilities, the research on direct instruction is so strongly supportive that this tactic demanded inclusion herein.

In preparation of this book, one issue with which I had to contend was which strategies to include and which to leave out. Although different scholars may disagree on specific instructional strategies as a "best practice," for students with learning disabilities, the research on direct instruction is so strongly supportive that this tactic demanded inclusion herein. Furthermore, for students with learning disabilities for whom no other reading or language arts tactic seems to work, the concerned teacher should obtain a direct instruction kit—these kits are probably available in your media center or through your local educational service unit—and try this strategy. For many students, the application of direct instruction techniques can—and often will—work miracles.

ASSESSMENT INNOVATIONS

Because of the importance of performance monitoring for students with learning disabilities, a number of innovative assessment approaches have been developed over the past decade, including performance assessment and portfolio assessment (Bryant, 1999; Gregory & Chapman, 2002, pp. 37-56). Although a complete exploration of these innovative concepts is beyond the scope of this text, some examples are provided below.

Performance Assessment

Performance assessment—which may also be referred to as authentic assessment—is based on the concept that students should produce actual products that are similar to products that would be produced in the "real world," and evaluation of the students' understanding should be based on those products or their performance in producing those products. Authentic tasks require that the student perform tasks in as realistic a fashion as possible, based on the context of the real world (Wiggins & McTighe, 1998). Below are several examples that have been used in various schools.

Knowledge of Late Middle Ages	Students may be required to plan, conduct, develop costumes for, and then perform a "King's Dinner." They must develop and dress in period costume, eat with the utensils used at that point (i.e., only a knife), speak some approximation of "Olde English," serve the school administrators the dinner with appropriate waitpersons, and so on.
Theme Writing	Students may be required to develop a campus newspaper, including news stories, various weekly columns, and so on, and produce an edition each week for the semester.
Studies of Ecosystems	Students may be required to sample water from several local creeks and rivers, testing for turbidity, microscopic life, and so on.

Clearly, these projects involve sophisticated understanding of the concepts that are typically taught in history, English, or science, but these concepts are applied in a real-world context. This aspect of performance assessment tends to make this instructional innovation into a rich

Kids enjoy acting out their learning.

teaching/learning experience, during which students actually experience the application of their growing knowledge in these fields. For this reason, many teachers become quite loyal to this teaching/assessment paradigm and consider it much more "fun" than traditional instruction.

Of course, not all performance assessment projects involve extensive classwide projects such as those described above. Less involved projects for individual students may be used for daily or weekly tasks. These may include the following:

Write a song or poem of a particular period

Draw a picture of a historical scene

Develop a model from toothpicks and glue

Illustrate a story

Teach a fifteen-minute period of class

Develop a multimedia report

As these projects suggest, the list of performance assessment projects is virtually endless, and the only limit is the creative imagination of the teacher. However, brainstorming various projects is merely the first step in performance assessment; teachers must also plan carefully what constitutes a finished performance and how those authentic assessments may be evaluated. Typically, in evaluating projects of this nature, a *rubric* (i.e., a specified set of evaluation criteria) is developed prior to the instructional exercise, and students are encouraged to compare their performance or product with the rubric continually throughout the work. Rubrics may be as extensive as necessary but should stipulate the specific components of the performance assessment project, as well as the relative grading "weight" of each component. In that fashion, students quickly realize what aspects of the project to emphasize.

REFLECTIVE EXERCISE: WRITING THE RUBRICS

One differentiated instructional exercise that can be based on a performance assessment model is involvement of the students in the initial planning of the performance-based product and in the writing of the grading rubric for that project. Could students in your class participate constructively in such an exercise, and would that lead to higher involvement with their learning if they helped to develop the project idea and the grading standards for it?

Portfolio Assessment

Another assessment innovation that has been incorporated into differentiated classes is the use of portfolios (Gregory & Chapman, 2002, pp. 50-54). A portfolio is a compilation of selected work by the student, which demonstrates the academic growth of the student over time and provides evidence of student accomplishment on particular skills. Portfolios encourage student ownership of the responsibility for the work and make the teacher and the student joint collaborators in the student's academic progress.

The portfolio should include work that the teacher and the student believe reflects the student's accomplishments most accurately. Students may include work that they are particularly proud of, that represents the most difficult task, or that represents a work in progress. Also, the portfolio should include an index prepared by the student as well as a reflective written document concerning why the student believes that this work represents his or her most important efforts. The index may be developed as an ongoing project with the portfolio, but the reflective essay should be completed prior to the end of the grading period.

Finally, the portfolio should include work from a student over a period of time and may include work from the first of the year as a comparison for work from the end of the year. All of these materials should be gathered and placed in some type of container (many teachers use an actual portfolio—hence the name—whereas others use small boxes). For both development and evaluation of the portfolio, a rubric should be developed with detailed indications of the level and scope of the work to be included within the portfolio, as well as the grading criteria to be used.

CONCLUSION

Students with learning disabilities require considerably more structure in their lessons than many other students, and monitoring students' academic performance on a daily basis can assist in providing much of the needed structure. Such monitoring will enable the student with the learning disability to see his or her performance in relation to previous efforts and to celebrate his or her growth toward the specific objectives on the IEP. For many students with learning disabilities, charting their performance is one of the most effective motivational tools teachers can employ.

This chapter has reviewed several strategies that are founded on this need for performance monitoring, including curriculum-based assessment, criterion-referenced testing, precision teaching, direct instruction, performance assessment, and portfolio assessment. Although there is considerable overlap between some of these strategies, application of any of these curriculum monitoring systems will increase the academic growth of students with learning disabilities in the inclusive class. Thus, one or more of these strategies should be incorporated into the IEP for almost every student with a learning disability.

What's Next?

With a variety of differentiated instructional tools covered in the first six chapters, the next chapter focuses on the single most frequently noted disability among students with learning disabilities—a problem in reading. Many of the instructional and assessment innovations described previously will be discussed in the context of various reading skills, and an emphasis will be placed on practical strategies that can be incorporated into almost every general education classroom.

7

Reading and Literacy Instruction for Students With Learning Disabilities

Strategies Included in This Chapter:

✔ A Literacy Checklist

✔ Phoneme-Based Lessons

✔ Word Recognition and Vocabulary Strategies:
    Picture Fading Strategy
    Word Bank Strategy
    Semantic Webs
    A Cloze Procedure

✔ Comprehension Strategies:
    A Repeated Reading Strategy
    A Storytelling Strategy
    A Prediction/Summarization Strategy
    Text Lookback Strategy

Almost every student diagnosed with a learning disability has some difficulty in reading, and these difficulties are most apparent in the general education classroom, where the child may be expected to perform the same work at the same reading level as his or her classmates. Although students with learning disabilities present a wide array of academic deficits, no deficit is as prevalent within the population of students with learning disabilities as deficits in reading. Furthermore, although math deficits or language deficits can certainly be debilitating, a deficit in reading is even more critical simply because this deficit will prevent learning in every other area (Kameenui, Carnine, Dixon, Simmons, & Coyne, 2002, pp. 1-40). For this reason, this chapter will present differentiated instructional strategies for teaching reading in the inclusive general education class. Because of the critical importance of reading for these children, every teacher, regardless of the grade level or instructional responsibility, should have access to differentiated instructional strategies for reading instruction.

Fortunately, research in the area of reading among students with learning disabilities has exploded within the past decade, with major advances in several related areas, including literacy instruction, phonological research, and reading intervention tactics (Chard & Dickson, 1999; Joseph, Noble, & Eden, 2001; Lyon & Moats, 1997). This chapter will briefly explore these areas to describe an array of specific instructional tactics that have been shown to be effective for students with learning disabilities in the general education setting.

WHAT IS LITERACY INSTRUCTION?

Many teachers in classrooms today may be unfamiliar with the emerging concept of literacy instruction; indeed, literacy instruction is a fairly new concept and incorporates more than merely the basal reading instruction procedures practiced by many of today's teachers. Literacy approaches focus not only on the phoneme-based instruction that students with learning disabilities need (Bos, Mather, Silver-Pacuilla, & Narr, 2000; Patzer & Pettegrew, 1996; Smith, Baker, & Oudeans, 2001) but also on the students' ability to speak, write, and listen effectively and to use these literacy skills in their daily work in a variety of school settings (Winn & Otis-Wilborn, 1999). The emphasis on a literacy approach is on the interrelationship between reading, writing, and language, and tactics such as storytelling that involve several of these areas are favored (i.e., using a language-based process to teach reading [see Craig, Hull, Haggart, & Crowder, 2001]; teachers will note that many of the strategies discussed in this chapter are effective for instruction in both reading and language arts). Furthermore, there is a growing emphasis on assisting struggling readers to improve their literacy, rather than focusing on remediation of specific reading deficits (Dayton-Sakari, 1997).

To make this concept of "literacy instruction" more concrete, we should review the various components of literacy. Smith et al. (2001) delineated several components of early literacy instruction that they felt constitute an effective literacy program. These include the following:

1. Allocation of time for daily, highly focused literacy instruction
2. Consistent routines for teaching the big ideas of literacy

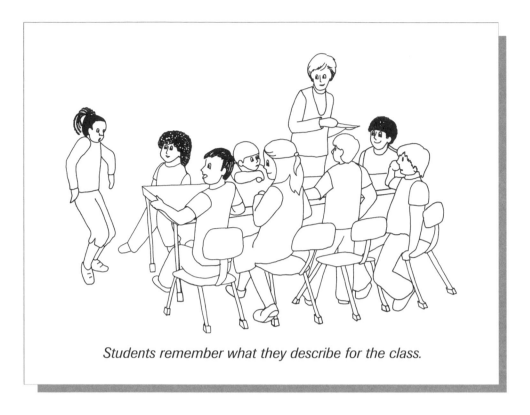

Students remember what they describe for the class.

3. Explicit instruction for new letter names and sounds

4. Daily "scaffolded" or assisted practice with auditory phoneme detection, segmenting, and blending

5. Immediate corrective feedback

6. Daily application of new knowledge at the phoneme and letter-sound levels across multiple and varied literacy contexts

7. Daily reviews

Of course, these components include some of the basic differentiated instruction concepts that have been presented previously in this text. For example, note the emphasis on scaffolded instruction and the focus on immediate corrective feedback. Thus, the "literacy" emphasis really is quite broad and encompasses a variety of ideas from other instructional paradigms; in point of fact, almost all instructional tactics for the differentiated classroom do! With these literacy components in mind, one may formulate a good understanding of what literacy instruction involves, and these components will provide something of a guideline to the topics discussed from this point on in the chapter.

Research on Literacy Instruction

Research on early literacy instruction for students with learning disabilities has been summarized in a variety of sources (Bos et al., 2000;

Kameenui et al., 2002, pp. 53-78; Patzer & Pettegrew, 1996; Smith et al., 2001). For example, the research has supported a strong phoneme-based instructional approach for students with learning disabilities and/or reading disabilities (Kameenui et al., 2002). Next, an emphasis on oral reading fluency is also recommended because students are often called on to read orally in class across the grade levels. Next, early instruction in reading should be quite robust; that is, instruction should be undertaken with sufficient intensity to assist students in reaching their early reading goals. Research has also shown that, for young readers who lag behind others in kindergarten and first grade, phonological instruction is even more important in their early literacy instruction. The good news from the research is that phonological awareness is a "teachable" skill, and adequate instruction in that area will enhance the reading of students—even older students—who display subsequent reading disabilities (Kameenui et al., 2002; Smith et al., 2001).

A Literacy Checklist

Literacy instructional tactics have been offered by a number of authors in the literature and generally reflect the entire array of reading skills ranging from early phonemic awareness to higher order reading comprehension (Bos et al., 2000; Smith et al., 2001; Winn & Otis-Wilborn, 1999). As one example, Winn and Otis-Wilborn (1999) suggested the use of individually developed checklists for monitoring the literacy of students with learning disabilities in the inclusive classroom. A sample of such a literacy checklist is presented in Teaching Tip 7.1. As you can see, this informal literacy checklist encompasses a wider variety of literacy skills than would a traditional reading instructional lesson, and this "broader view" is the perspective supported by proponents of literacy instruction. Of course, teachers should vary the reading skills on the checklist for each student with a learning disability to reflect specifically those literacy skills that are relevant for that particular student.

Phonological Awareness

One aspect of early literacy instruction that is heavily emphasized is phonological awareness (Kameenui et al., 2002). In fact, within the past decade, research has documented that phonological awareness is both a critical component of many subsequent language arts and literacy skills (Bos et al., 2000; Chard & Dickson, 1999), as well as a primary deficit area for many students with learning disabilities (Kameenui et al., 2002; Moats & Lyon, 1993). Based on recent research, a general consensus has emerged that students with learning disabilities demonstrate an early inability to manipulate phonemes, and this inability is the primary cause of subsequent learning disabilities in a wide variety of areas (Moats & Lyon, 1993). For this reason, it is critical that every general education

☞ **Teaching Tip 7.1**

A Literacy Checklist

Name _____ Date _____

Type of Activity: _____ oral reading   _____ studying text
                  _____ group reading   _____ other

Reading Material _____

_____

Attempts to Decode Unknown Words _____

_____

Uses Context Clues_____

_____

Summarizes Plot/Character Information_____

_____

Uses Personal Experiences _____

_____

Notes Sequences of Events _____

_____

Demonstrates Self-Checking_____

_____

Other Comments: _____

_____

teacher in the lower grades understand the concept of phonological awareness and have access to several phonological awareness instructional strategies.

Phonological awareness, though intimately related to phonics, is not the same as phonics (Chard & Dickson, 1999). Whereas phonics involves the relationship between letters and their related sounds, phonological awareness represents the ability to detect and manipulate discrete sounds, and thus phonemic manipulation skills precede skills in phonics. Furthermore, there is a hierarchy of phonemic manipulation skills that students must master (Kameenui et al., 2002, p. 58). For example, most theorists suggest that detecting similar sounds (rhyming) is a phonemic skill that precedes detecting different initial sounds (i.e., the difference between the first sound in *cat* vs. *hat*). This continuum of phonemic skills varies somewhat from one researcher to another, but the following sequence of skills represents this concept.

Detecting rhyming sounds	Various rhyming exercises may be used
Isolating initial sounds	What is the first sound in *ball?*
Isolating middle/ending sounds	What is the last sound in *house?*
Blending sounds into words	What word do you have if you put these sounds together (ho-may-ker)?
Segmenting or dividing sounds within words	What do the parts of this word sound like if you divide it up? (banana)
Changing/manipulating sounds	What would *cat* sound like if you put an "ha" sound in front?

Of course, after a student can manipulate sounds in this fashion, the student must be trained in the alphabetic principle (sometimes referred to as the alphabetic code)—the idea that the forty-four different phonemes in the English language may be represented by twenty-six letters or combinations of those twenty-six letters (Sousa, 2001b). This instruction in the alphabetic code is referred to as phonics and involves a process of mapping speech sounds to written or printed letters. Thus, phonics instruction proceeds only after a student has mastered phonemic awareness and phonemic manipulation (Kameenui et al., 2002, pp. 58-65). Furthermore, students must learn letter sounds and these phonemic manipulation skills to a very high level of automaticity to learn to read fluently.

With this distinction between phonics and phonological instruction noted, it is immediately apparent that merely teaching students "letter sounds" may not be enough for students with learning disabilities because those students may not be able to discriminate between the various letter sounds anyway! Thus, instructional activities in phonological awareness skills are necessary for many students with learning disabilities (Smith, 1998). Typically, phonological instruction would precede instruction in phonics itself and may begin as early as prekindergarten. However, for students who have not mastered phonemic awareness and manipulation skills, even as late as elementary grades and middle school, this instruction must precede higher level instruction in reading (Kameenui et al., 2002, pp. 50-65).

Phonological Instructional Ideas

Phonological instruction can involve a wide variety of instructional activities such as rhyming word activities, hunt for sound-alike word activities, or sound blending. To give teachers a better sense of how phonological skills may be taught, here are two examples that would be appropriate for the inclusive class. First, a series of sample instructional activities that emphasize sounds and sound-blending activities are presented in Teaching Tip 7.2.

Next, Kameenui and his coworkers (2002, p. 68) recommended a series of instructional scaffolds, presented below, designed to support students in learning phonological recognition skills. Note the similarity between these activities and the metacognitive/scaffolded approach described earlier.

Scaffold 1—Model	The teacher says the sounds in a word while touching each letter: "My turn to sound out this word. When I touch a letter, I'll say its sound. I'll keep saying the sound until I touch the next letter."
Scaffold 2—Overt sound out	The teacher touches under each letter while students say each sound: "Your turn to sound out this word. When I touch a letter, you say its sound. Keep saying the sound until I touch the next letter."
Scaffold 3—Internal sound out	The teacher touches under each letter while students say each sound in their head: "You are going to read this word without saying the sounds out loud. As I point to the letters, sound out this word to yourself."
Scaffold 4—Whole-word reading	The teacher points to the word and students sound it out independently: "You are going to read this word the fast way. When I point to a word, sound it out to yourself. When I signal, say the word the fast way."

👉 Teaching Tip 7.2

Sample Phonological Activities and Lesson Plans

Guess the Word Game Lesson

Objective: Students will be able to blend and identify a word that is stretched out into component sounds.

Materials needed: Picture cards of objects that students are likely to recognize, such as sun, bell, fan, flag, snake, tree, book, cup, clock, and plane.

Activity: Place a small number of picture cards before children. Tell them you are going to say a word using "snail talk"—a slow way of saying words (e.g., fffff lllll aaaaa ggggg). They have to look at the pictures and guess what the snail is saying. It is important to have the children guess the answer in their head so that everyone gets an opportunity to try it before hearing other answers. Alternate between having one child identify the word and having all children say the word aloud in chorus to keep the children engaged.

Segmentation Lesson

Objective: Students will be able to segment various parts of oral language.

Materials needed: List of brief phrases or poems children would know (e.g., "I scream. You scream. We all scream for ice cream").

Activities:

(a) Early instruction involves teaching the children to segment sentences into individual words. Have the children clap their hands with each individual word.

(b) As children advance, teach them to segment words into syllables. You may wish to start with children's names (Al-ex-an-der; Ra-chel).

(c) When children have learned to remove the first phoneme from a word, teach them to segment short words into individual phonemes (s-u-n: s-t-o-p).

Change the Letter Game

Objective: Students will be able to detect the letter change and pronounce the word with the substitute letter.

Materials needed: List of word cards, each of which presents a simple noun with three letters and a picture of that object (consonant-vowel-consonant words; e.g., *bat, cup, hat, ham,* etc.).

Activities: Students: "Mr. Sound will show you a word and then will change the first letter of the word." (Show a picture of a bat.) "Say this word together." (Students say *bat.*) "Mr. Sound wants to change the first sound to an *h.*" (Teacher says the letter sound for *h* and not the letter name.) "If Mr. Sound changes that sound, what would be the matching picture?" Encourage each student to decide on the answer prior to calling on a student for the answer.

SOURCE: These ideas were adapted from "Phonological Awareness: Instructional and Assessment Guidelines" by Chard, D. J., & Dickson, S. V. (1999). *Intervention in School and Clinic,* 34, 261-270. ©1999 by PRO-ED, Inc. Adapted with permission.

REFLECTIVE EXERCISE: LITERACY INSTRUCTION VERSUS READING INSTRUCTION

Pretend that you are explaining the concept of literacy instruction to a parent. Describe how this approach may differ from traditional basal reading approaches in terms of the scope of the instructional activities, as well as the emphasis on reading as related to other skill areas.

STRATEGIES FOR WORD RECOGNITION

Beyond merely understanding phonemes and specific letter sounds, students must have the ability to decode unknown words to read. Furthermore, understanding the meaning of words in reading material is fundamental to the overall goal of comprehending the meaning of the text. Consequently, many strategies for teaching word decoding, word attack, and word comprehension have been proposed. This section presents a series of strategies whereby word attack skills may be taught to students with learning disabilities.

Sight Word and Vocabulary Instruction

Sight word strategies do not involve decoding or "sounding out" unknown words. Rather, sight word instruction involves learning words in other ways. Use of word configuration or the shape of the word (e.g., boxes drawn around the letters in the word *bottle*) would be a common sight-word recognition technique. Other word instruction tactics for use with students with learning disabilities may include picture fading and various word bank activities.

Picture Fading. Picture fading is built on the concept of paired associate learning or pairing stimuli together; a picture is paired with the noun it represents, and the student is exposed to both simultaneously. Subsequently, the picture is gradually faded out (Corry & Shamow, 1972; Dorry, 1976; Knowlton, 1980). The picture-fading technique usually involves a series of cards with a word-picture pair on each card. The cards may then be placed on a handheld "picture fading board" to which several pieces of translucent plastic are attached. The plastic allows the teacher to cover the picture without covering the word. The teacher asks the student to pronounce one of several such words and then covers the picture associated with each word with one sheet of plastic. This plastic partially "fades" the picture from view, leaving the word in plain sight, and after several pieces of plastic cover the picture, the pictures are faded entirely. Complete fading usually takes five to seven trials.

Picture-fading techniques work best with lower level words—typically nouns—during the early grades, although this technique may be appropriate for content pictures in upper grade levels. Nouns are easier to "picture" than other types of words, but a creative teacher may find interesting ways to draw certain action words. Many teachers apply this technique by drawing or locating pictures of common household and classroom objects and then making picture-fading cards for them.

A Rebus Approach. The rebus approach to reading and word recognition for young children involves substitution of pictures for words in sentences to be read, as in the illustrated sentence below.

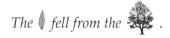

The ⧫ fell from the 🌳.

In some examples, the words are placed in the sentence in addition to the picture, and eventually the picture would be dropped. Like the picture-fading strategy presented earlier, this is another form of paired associate learning. The correct word identification is facilitated by teaching the use of picture clues that accompany each stimulus. Many parents may recall use of this approach with their own children during preschool reading at bedtime. This is an effective technique for students, even before they have been introduced to the alphabet, and many books are available to parents in toy stores and book stores that use this approach.

Word Bank Instruction. Many teachers use a word bank, in which five to ten unknown sight words are enclosed and used for an instructional activity of some type each day. Generally, the teacher begins by having the student read a word list, which may be either a list of sight words or a list of vocabulary words from a subject content text. The teacher marks the errors and stops the child when ten words have been misread. A mark is made under the last word attempted, and that line is dated; the page is filed and will be used again as an informal assessment measure. The ten unknown words are written on cardboard (or light paper stock) and become the student's word bank. The cards can then be placed in a word can. Although any type of personal container will do, I used the cardboard "potato chip cans" and had the junior high students in my class decorate their individual word cans. Although many teachers use word bank activities for teaching sight words, I had junior high–age students use word bank activities to learn subject content words from their subject area classes. This is a great activity in which the special education teacher can support the content of the inclusive class.

Daily word bank activities may include having the student write each word several times and read them to the teacher. On other days, the students may look up their words, use them in sentences, use them in a story, or locate them in a story. The critical aspect of the word bank tactic is that the student must use each word in the word bank each day for one task or another. After about two weeks, the student will be able to read these words with very little problem. At that point, the student is told to take the words home and share them with his or her parents. The word list is used again, and another ten words are selected for the word bank. For higher level students learning content area words, you may change words in the word bank as the units of instruction change in the inclusive class.

At the end of the year, the student will have learned a large number of new words, and the teacher will be able to show to the parents the word list, which indicates specifically the vocabulary level of the student at the first of the year and the succeeding mastery of various groups of words throughout the year. Parents generally respond quite favorably to specific evidence of academic growth, such as that represented by this word list. Teaching Tip 7.3 presents additional word bank activities that may be completed using these words. Also, precision teaching provides one of the best methods for monitoring progress on sight word recognition for word bank activities. Such a project is presented in Teaching Tip 7.4.

Word Attack Strategies

Because of the regularity of word pronunciation in English and the general rules of word formation, several specific word attack skills can be of benefit in decoding new words for students with reading disabilities. In fact, approximately 85% of words in English are "regular"; that is, these words may be decoded using phonics as well as a set of specified word attack rules. Although phonics instruction involves instruction on pronunciation of many words, a complete description of the rules of and instructional techniques for phonics is not appropriate herein simply because general education teachers teaching above the second grade will rarely spend any time in phonics instruction. However, in addition to phonics skills, other word attack skills such as structural analysis and syllabication are very appropriate for the inclusive class in the higher grades.

Syllabication. The ability to divide a multisyllabic word into syllables enhances a student's ability to read unknown words in at least two ways. First, syllables are easier to read than longer words for many students with learning disabilities. Next, syllabication allows for the subsequent phonetic decoding of each syllable. Because syllabication makes the use of phonics possible, an inability to divide words into syllables can greatly hamper a student's reading efforts. For this reason, teachers across the grade levels should stress syllabication skills.

Teaching Tip 7.3

Activities for Word Bank Words

1. Look for words that have the same spelling.
2. Look for words that rhyme.
3. Look for words that may mean the same thing (i.e., synonyms).
4. Write words on cards and play a "dominoes" game by matching the first two or the last two letters of each word.
5. Categorize words by their type: nouns, pronouns, verbs, and so on.
6. Have students write stories together using all of their words.

 Teaching Tip 7.4

Precision Teaching Project on Sight Word Recognition

This tip describes a precision teaching project used to monitor sight word recognition for a student with a learning disability. This type of project works well, regardless of the specific types of activities the child uses each day to study his or her words from the word bank. First, as described above, the teacher should identify only those words the student does not know. Approximately ten words should go in the word bank. To get an accurate count on reading rate for the ten words in the word can, the teacher must prepare a reading sheet that lists those ten words in random order, with each word listed at least ten times. This should provide enough words for the child to be able to continue reading through a one-minute or two-minute period. After the child's word bank activity for the day is finished, the teacher and the child sit together, and at the beginning of the timing period, the child begins to read the words. During this timed reading activity, the child reads as many words as possible in the allotted time. Words read correctly and errors are counted and charted; the teacher should mark corrections and errors on another sheet.

After the student reaches his or her goal, the teacher should change the words in the word bank. If a word has proven to be particularly hard, it may be kept, along with nine new words. Of course, each change of words should be indicated as a phase change line on the precision teaching chart, as described in Chapter 6.

☞ **Teaching Tip 7.5**

Common Syllabication Rules

1. When two consonants come between two vowels, as in *hammer* and *slumber*, divide the word between the two consonants: *ham/mer, slum/ber.*

2. When a single consonant comes between the two vowels, divide the word after the first vowel: *be/gan.*

3. When a word ends in a consonant followed by *le*, as in *table*, the final syllable is made up of the consonant and the *le: ta/ble.*

4. Generally, multiletter suffixes are syllables by themselves: *head/ed, load/ing.*

A number of syllabication rules are generally applicable and may be taught as general guidelines for reading even in higher grades in the content area classes. Although no single set of rules is comprehensive enough to cover every situation in English, several of the most common rules for syllabication are presented in Teaching Tip 7.5 above.

Syllabication skills are generally taught using these general rules, and students with learning disabilities can usually master these rules once specific and explicit instruction is provided. Teachers should make a chart of these rules and place it permanently in the classroom. In fact, one may think of these rules as a metacognitive strategy that enables a student to recognize the likely positions of syllables in words. Instruction would proceed, as described in Chapter 4, by eliciting cooperation and modeling the rule application with known words, application to unknown words, and daily checks of progress. The creative teacher may even identify an acronym to represent each of these rules.

Structural Analysis. For students with learning disabilities beyond Grade 3, the use of structural analysis of words is recommended. Structural analysis involves direct instruction in the ability to recognize prefixes, suffixes, and root words. For example, the word *playing* looks considerably longer and more complicated to many third graders than the more common word *play.* Indeed, for some students with learning disabilities, such a multisyllabic word may seem quite intimidating. However, identification of the suffix syllable *-ing* will aid those students in recognition of the word.

Teaching the most common prefixes and suffixes will thus assist in the overall reading performance for most students with learning

---

> **Teaching Tip 7.6**
>
> ### A Visual Scan Worksheet for Locating Prefixes/Suffixes
>
> Directions: You should look at each word, identify the prefix or suffix, and circle it.
>
> | | | | |
> |---|---|---|---|
> | fighting | write | coming | subtopic |
> | women | using | taken | learned |
> | home | restless | prohibit | habit |
> | insight | beside | before | sightless |
> | desks | chair | table | insight |
>
> This listing could also include more advanced suffixes and prefixes. Also, a worksheet such as this would be appropriate for use on a timed precision teaching task to document mastery of suffixes and prefixes.

---

disabilities, and most general education teachers spend some time on word structure. Various strategies may be used to which prefixes and suffixes are taught. Teaching Tip 7.6 above presents a worksheet that uses a visual scanning technique to identify prefixes and suffixes. Teachers may use this model with other lists of words and develop a series of worksheets stressing structural analysis. Completion of this type of worksheet on a daily basis would result in a total number of correct answers and errors that could then be plotted on a precision teaching chart for evaluation of the student's performance.

A Structural Analysis Learning Strategy. As discussed in Chapter 4, the University of Kansas researchers have produced a number of learning strategies to assist students with learning disabilities perform various tasks. The DISSECT strategy (Bryant, Ugel, Thompson, & Hamff, 1999; Ellis, 1994; Lenz, Schumaker, Deshler, & Beals, 1984) was developed to enable secondary students to identify the meaning of unknown words in text. This strategy would be presented to the students in the same fashion as discussed in Chapter 4, including presentation of the strategy, modeling, teaching of known words, application of the strategy to unknown words, and generalization of the strategy. For students with learning disabilities who have difficulty with structural analysis, this tactic would be applicable in almost every general education class. Teaching Tip 7.7 presents the steps in the DISSECT strategy.

☞ **Teaching Tip 7.7**

The DISSECT Learning Strategy

D   Discover the word's context. Reread the sentence before and after the word. Look at the pictures.

I   Isolate the prefix. Look for common prefixes the student already knows.

S   Separate the suffix.

S   Say the stem. See if the stem is recognizable in isolation (without prefix or suffix).

E   Examine the stem. If the stem is not immediately recognizable, the student may have to sound it out or at least sound out the pronounceable parts.

C   Check with someone. If the student has some idea of the word, he or she should check that out.

T   Try the dictionary. If a student has no one to ask, or if that person doesn't know, the dictionary should be referred to.

SOURCE: Adapted from Ellis (1994) and Bryant, Ugel, Thompson, and Hamff (1999). See also Lenz and Hughes (1990) and Lenz, Schumaker, Deshler, and Beals (1984).

NOTE: Training in this and other learning strategies instruction is available through the University of Kansas, Lawrence (phone: 913-864-4780 for information).

WORD COMPREHENSION

Whereas the techniques reviewed earlier concentrated basically on recognition of words, the following techniques address the issue of word comprehension in text. In some of the strategies, correct pronunciation of the word is not addressed because the skill is seen as less important than deriving meaning from the word in context. There are numerous methods that address word comprehension. Some of these are useful for lower level readers in the earlier grades, whereas other techniques may be used in higher grade levels in subject content areas.

A Semantic Webbing Strategy

Many students with learning disabilities have difficulty in vocabulary as well as difficulty in detecting the relationships between the concepts in their reading assignments, and those relationships often represent the basis of higher order understandings. Both the student's vocabulary, as well as the student's sense of relationships between concepts, may be strengthened by using a semantic web for most reading

Teaching Tip 7.8

Semantic Web

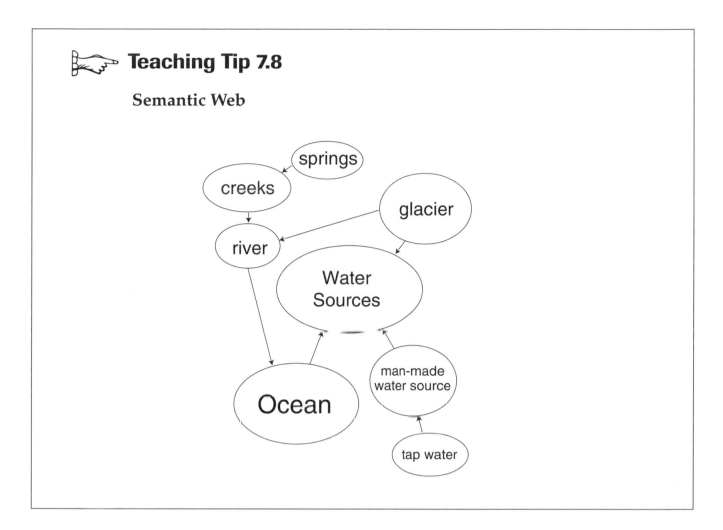

assignments (this same tactic is sometimes referred to as *semantic maps*) (see Bos et al., 2000; Bryant et al., 1999).

A *semantic web* may be considered a scaffold for student learning. Typically, the web presents a word or a phrase, written in a central circle on the dry-erase board or worksheet, and the activity involves having the students and the teacher together determine what other words relate to the central word, as presented in Teaching Tip 7.8. Those additional terms and concepts are written on the board in separate circles and placed in proximity to each other as dictated by the underlying relationships between them. The emphasis is on meaningful relationships, and some teachers in developing the semantic web write in each circle not only the related term but also an abbreviated rationale describing the relationship between the new term and the central term in the web.

In the example above, the term *creeks* is related to "rivers" and thereby to the central term *water sources,* but because creeks rarely flow directly into the ocean, there is no relationship depicted directly from "creek" to "ocean." As this example illustrates, the semantic web is one literacy instructional concept that can be used across the grade levels and in a variety of topical areas. For students with learning disabilities, each reading assignment may be the opportunity to develop a semantic web, and for students of differing ability levels, the teacher may differentiate the instruction by supplying some of the terms for the web, placed in their appropriate positions.

A Cloze Procedure

A *cloze procedure* is a structured fill-in-the-blank activity that emphasizes word comprehension and use of context clues. This tactic may be used across the grade levels and in a variety of subject areas. Teaching Tip 7.9 presents an example of a cloze procedure.

In using a cloze procedure, the semantic and syntactic clues embedded within the reading passage serve as an aid in the student's selection of the correct content term, which would then be used to fill in the blank. For many students with learning disabilities, this can be a very effective reading technique. Inclusive class teachers can form a cloze procedure reading activity from almost any reading section by selecting every seventh content word (i.e., omitting words such as *a*, *and*, and *the* from the count of words) and deleting these content terms. In contrast, teachers may merely select a reading passage and choose random content words to replace with a blank line. Not only does this force the students to read the words, but this tactic also forces students with learning disabilities to attend to the content of the reading passage to interpret the context clues. Of course, prior to use with students, the newly prepared reading selection should be checked to ensure that the blanks may be completed by use of the available clues.

As an alternative, this cloze procedure activity can easily be modified in inclusive classes for students with learning disabilities merely by providing a "word list" from which the correct terms may be selected. These terms would then be matched to the particular blanks in the reading selection by the students.

As a final step, teachers may wish to adapt a series of cloze procedure reading activities into a daily precision teaching instructional project. For students with learning disabilities, reading a prepared reading selection of this nature every day would quickly yield information on their progress in building the vocabulary for that unit of instruction. Again, the daily scores for correct and incorrect answers should be charted to demonstrate progress. This activity is particularly appropriate for use in the late elementary and higher grades to teach vocabulary particular to the subject area. Historically, this cloze procedure has been used to assess passage comprehension, though "comprehension of words in text" may be a more accurate description of this particular skill.

Teaching Tip 7.9

A Cloze Procedure for Reading Instruction

I remember visiting my grandparents on their farm way out in the _____. They raised corn and oats, and the farm was also a noisy home to many animals. Each morning, before I got out of _____ I could hear the _____ crow at first light. Shortly after those morning noises, I would hear the _____ mooing, as my grandfather began milking them. Making the farm even noisier, the dog always seemed to be _____. Mornings were noisy times at Grandfather's _____.

 REFLECTIVE EXERCISE:
THE CLOZE PROCEDURE AS THE
DEFINITIVE COMPREHENSION EXERCISE

Reflect on the various ways educators measure reading comprehension (e.g., read a passage and then answer written questions, read a passage and then point to a picture that it describes, etc.). For many researchers, the cloze procedure is the most effective way to measure comprehension, simply because the comprehension exercise is embedded within the reading itself and is not exclusively a postreading activity. This makes the cloze procedure more similar to actual reading comprehension. Can you think of other ways to measure comprehension that are more directly tied to the written text?

READING STRATEGIES FOR THE ELEMENTARY AND MIDDLE GRADES

A number of instructional tactics for enhancing reading comprehension have been described previously in this chapter and in this text. However, a number of additional tactics are described below that are particularly effective for reading instruction in the elementary and middle grades, both for increasing reading fluency or reading comprehension (Bryant et al., 1999; Mastropieri, Leinart, & Scruggs, 1999; Swanson & De La Paz, 1998).

A Prediction/Summarization Tactic

Students with learning disabilities approach a reading task differently than normal readers, in that they neither predict what is likely to come next in a reading selection nor summarize their reading to monitor and enhance their comprehension (Bryant et al., 1999). In short, many students with learning disabilities, particularly in oral reading activities, merely "say the words" without truly understanding that they should be deriving understanding from the text. Thus, strategies that assist students with learning disabilities to mentally get involved and interact with their reading material will assist these readers. Specifically, strategies should encourage students to do the following:

1. Predict what the reading passage is likely to contain
2. Summarize the passage to monitor comprehension

These two strategies are likely to result in higher levels of comprehension; in fact, both prediction and summarizing were emphasized in the reciprocal teaching strategy described in Chapter 4. When assigning a reading selection to students with learning disabilities, teachers should emphasize prediction and summarization by using a worksheet that the student must complete during the reading process. A sample prediction/summarization worksheet is presented in Teaching Tip 7.10, and you can easily adapt this prediction/summarization worksheet for a wide variety of reading tasks across the grade levels. This tactic will assist students with learning disabilities to become more involved in the reading content.

A Repeated Readings Tactic

Some students with learning disabilities are very reluctant to read orally in content area classes because of the slow speed of their reading. In fact, oral reading often results in embarrassment for these students in elementary classrooms, and the students, in effect, learn to hate reading. For this reason, every general education teacher in inclusive classes should use a technique that will assist these students in oral reading fluency.

Research on the repeated readings tactic has documented that repeated readings are effective for increasing reading fluency for students with learning disabilities in the elementary grades as well as middle school and high school (see Mastropieri et al., 1999, for a brief review of this research). Various researchers have used this strategy, with some

☞ Teaching Tip 7.10

A Prediction/Summarization Tactic

Before Reading

What is the story title? _____

_____

What content predictions can I make based on that? _____

_____

Are there pictures that suggest the topic? _____

_____

What do I want to learn about that topic? _____

_____

During Reading

What is the main idea or problem? _____

_____

How was the problem managed? _____

_____

After Reading

Was the problem successfully dealt with? _____

_____

What is the main story or lesson? _____

_____

What did I learn? _____

_____

having students repeatedly read the same passage up to seven times to improve reading fluency prior to orally reading the passage in class. However, having a student with a learning disability read the same passage three times is more typical and works quite well. Of course, the reading passages must be presented at the appropriate instructional level for the student with the learning disabilities; a student should be able to read a minimum of 80% of the words correctly initially, and the student should be expected to repeatedly read the passage until he or she reaches the criteria of 95%. Also, help with unknown words should be offered as the student is reading the passage.

Research has demonstrated that students with learning disabilities can improve their oral reading fluency when the repeated reading tactic is used. Mastropieri and her coworkers (1999) offer several additional guidelines for using this tactic, as presented in Teaching Tip 7.11.

REFLECTIVE EXERCISE: TIME TO READ

As critical a skill as reading is, many teachers may view the repeated reading strategy described above as too expensive in terms of the student's time. How can any teacher in any busy classroom find the time to monitor a student reading the same text three or four times as a repeated reading activity? A moment's reflection can dissipate that concern. First, no activity in school is as important as a student learning to read, and strategies in this field must supercede all other instruction. Next, using a buddy system or peer tutoring as described previously gives teachers a way to implement this repeated reading strategy while not having to spend all of their time with one student. Teachers should reflect on the importance of this idea and jot down a few ideas for implementing this strategy as they move toward a more differentiated classroom.

READING IN THE CONTENT AREAS

Reading in content areas is quite different from reading stories in the elementary grades. Content area readings from textbooks are likely to be more highly related across days than are the stories in the basal reading series in the elementary classroom. Chapters of reading material in content areas tend to be related in a sequential way in almost every subject (e.g., studies of the Revolution precede studies of the Federalist period, and studies of invertebrates precede studies of vertebrates). Thus, students need to understand the differences in these reading assignments, as well as the relationships across chapters in content area reading.

Teaching Tip 7.11

Ten Steps for Implementing a Repeated Reading Tactic

1. The teacher should explain to the student how reading practice will help the student read more fluently; this will typically lead to less embarrassment in inclusive classes for many students with learning disabilities and/or reading problems. Most students with learning disabilities will be highly motivated to use this tactic, if it is presented in this fashion.

2. The teacher and each student with a learning disability should select an appropriate reading rate goal, and each goal should be stated in terms of words read correctly per minute.

3. Based on the reading instructional level for each individual student (i.e., the reading level at which the student accurately reads a minimum of 85% of the words correctly), the teacher and the student should select reading passages for use in the repeated reading tactic.

4. The teacher should calculate the reading rates for each student (a review of the precision teaching tactic described in Chapter 6 will help here).

5. The teacher should also teach each student how to calculate, record, and interpret his or her own reading rates.

6. Tell the students to choose a story that interests them and practice reading the story or reading selection alone (or with a buddy, if you wish to use the buddy system) three times.

7. Students should be encouraged to ask for help in pronouncing words when needed during the first three readings or practice readings. This will assist them in learning the new terms.

8. After practicing three times, the student should read the story again, as fast as possible, while using a stopwatch or clock with a second hand to time himself or herself.

9. After the final reading, the student should record the time on a graph.

10. The student should be encouraged to compare that performance with the reading rate goal set earlier and also with previous performance.

Several strategies can assist in content area reading in the elementary, middle, and upper grades.

A Text Lookback Tactic

One idea that will assist older students with learning disabilities in their reading summarization in content area reading is instruction in "text lookbacks" (Swanson & De La Paz, 1998). In using a text lookback tactic, teachers should directly teach the skills involved in looking back over a text chapter or assigned reading to find specific information. When partnered with a set of specific comprehension questions, the ability to look back in the text to find answers to the questions will greatly assist students with learning disabilities in comprehension of the assigned reading material.

Some general education teachers may assume that telling students with learning disabilities to "look back over the chapter and find the answer" is sufficient for those students. However, the fact is that there are a number of different skills involved in looking back through a chapter for specific information, and many students with learning disabilities in the middle and upper grades do not know how to search for answers to questions in the textbook. At a minimum, these text lookback skills would involve the following:

1. Remembering when certain information was covered—early or late in the chapter

2. Using headings to find the right section of text

3. Reading topic sentences under the appropriate heading

4. Identifying a specific paragraph where the answer might be

5. Finding the answer in that chapter or continuing the search

Swanson and De La Paz (1998) encouraged teachers to directly model this text lookback strategy for their students while verbally rehearsing the skills. These authors suggested the dialogue presented in Teaching Tip 7.12 as a model instructional lesson for teaching text lookback skills to students with learning disabilities.

The Verbal Retelling Tactic

Many strategies for increasing comprehension today emphasize the students' telling or retelling what they have read (Craig et al., 2001; Ward-Lonergan, Liles, & Anderson, 1999). In fact, verbally retelling the information from a story, a reading passage, or even a lecture in a subject content area has been shown to increase comprehension among students with learning disabilities in the middle and upper grades (Ward-Lonergan et al., 1999). Verbally retelling the main information helps a student focus on the important aspects of the information presented and thus represents one method by which a student may summarize the information in the text. For this reason, middle and upper grade teachers in the general education classroom should frequently require students to retell information that has just been read or otherwise presented in class. When a selection is read, either silently or orally in the class, the teacher may invite students to retell the important aspects of the reading selection by saying something like the following:

☞ **Teaching Tip 7.12**

Teaching a Text Lookback Strategy

In teaching a text lookback strategy, the teacher should directly model the lookback strategy and "think out loud." The teacher might say something like. . . .

> The question is asking us which mountains separate France from Spain. I don't remember, so I'll look back in the chapter until I find it. First, I'll skim over the chapter until I come to the section where I think I'll find the answer. The first section of the chapter is about the history of France, so the answer wouldn't be there. The second section talks about the people and culture, so that answer wouldn't be there. The next section is about the landscape. I think that the answer will be here somewhere, so I'll start to look a little more carefully. The first part talks about rivers, so I'm not going to worry about that. The next part talks about mountains. This is where the answer will be, so I will read this paragraph carefully. Here we go; it says that in the southwest, the Pyrenees separate France from Spain. So my answer to the question is the Pyrenees.

SOURCE: From "Teaching Effective Comprehension Strategies to Students With Learning and Reading Disabilities" by Swanson, P. N., & De La Paz, S. (1998). *Intervention in School and Clinic,* *33*(4), 209-218. ©1998 by PRO-ED, Inc. Adapted with permission.

> Now we're going to work together to retell the information we just read. You may refer to your books as you need to. I'd like for someone to tell me the names of the persons we just read about, and then I'll call on someone else to tell me the first thing that happened.

With this type of "team" approach, it will be easier to get students with learning disabilities to participate in retelling a part of the reading passage. Also, teachers can strengthen this activity by having another student summarize the main points of the passage on the dry-erase board in outline form. Subsequent to the retelling, teachers may call on yet another student with a learning disability to review that outline for the class and add to it as necessary.

I have personally used a more structured "retelling" approach for both reading and listening to lectures in higher level classes called the RTC procedure. RTC stands for "recorder, talker, and checker." Prior to beginning a ten- to fifteen-minute segment of a lecture, I appoint students for the following jobs:

R—a *recorder*, who records the critical information on a poster as I lecture,

T—a *talker*, who will present that critical information to the class at the end of my twenty-minute presentation, and

C—a *checker*, who checks to ensure that the critical information is all covered by the recorder and the talker.

Thus, after I present information for a while, I then have students in the class present the critical aspects of the information I just covered. This ensures participation of the students who are serving in these roles and breaks up the lecture/discussion format. Also, sometimes teachers do not say exactly what they wish to say, and/or students hear something different, so this procedure gives the teacher the opportunity to hear what the students heard and to correct, clarify, or add to that information. This is a fairly simple retelling procedure that teachers from Grade 4 through secondary school can easily implement in inclusive classes.

> Verbally retelling the information from a story, a reading passage, or even a lecture in a subject content area has been shown to increase comprehension among students with learning disabilities in the middle and upper grades.

A Storytelling Tactic

Closely allied with the retelling tactic described above is the use of *storytelling* in reading and language instruction (Craig et al., 2001). Storytelling involves the teacher, another adult, or a student in using language to present a narrative to the class. When a teacher is telling a story, the structure of the story itself provides a perfect opportunity for the teacher to "coach" the student and his or her listeners in the structure of narratives. For example, after the teacher describes the characters involved and sets up the story "problem" or plot, the teacher could ask students to predict what may come next (i.e., the anticipated climax). Coaching on story structure can enhance reading across the subject areas because understanding the story structure is a critical reading skill.

There are a number of other advantages in using storytelling in reading and language arts instruction. First, having students of various ethnic backgrounds tell stories offers the opportunity to explore the cultural diversity that is so characteristic in today's classrooms (Craig et al., 2001). Next, teachers may find that students with learning disabilities can demonstrate knowledge of the subject matter more effectively in a storytelling format than on the unit test. Thus, this tactic may well provide teachers in inclusive classes with an alternative testing format. Finally, storytelling involves multiple language capabilities on the part of the student with a learning disability. These include the following:

Language ability

Understanding of story components

Use of facial cues, voice tone, and physical gestures for enhancing the interest level (i.e., "dramatic license")

Understanding of cues from one's audience

These and many other aspects of communications are involved in the act of telling a story. Because of the involvement in these multiple skills, storytelling is truly a "literacy" strategy rather than a "reading" strategy per se. Teaching Tip 7.13 presents ten tactics that may be used to employ storytelling in your classroom.

CONCLUSION

In this chapter, perhaps more so than others in this text, the overlap of various strategies is quite apparent. Because reading is a deficit area for many students with learning disabilities, it has become one of the most thoroughly researched areas in the field, and there are numerous instructional strategies that will facilitate differentiated instruction for students with learning disabilities and others in the class. This chapter has presented the growing emphasis on a holistic approach—literacy instruction—that seems to encompass many of the techniques for teaching reading, and although many more specific strategies are available in the literature, the array of strategies presented here does demonstrate the types of strategies that general education teachers are using to differentiate instruction for students with learning disabilities in the inclusive classes. These ideas and teaching procedures will greatly assist all students in those classes and are essential for the reading success of students with learning disabilities.

What's Next?

Although this chapter and text have presented a large number of strategies for differentiating instruction in the classroom, teachers may wonder where to begin. The final chapter suggests how teachers may wish to move into differentiated instruction in their own class.

☞ Teaching Tip 7.13

Ten Tactics for Using Storytelling to Teach Reading

1. Whenever possible, the teacher should use storytelling to illustrate events in history, science, or other subject areas. Rather than telling how scared the soldiers were just prior to the last day of the battle of Gettysburg, the teacher may use a storytelling technique to make that event "real" for the students. Even parts of books read to the students can present these historical facts (e.g., using a few pages of the popular book *Killer Angels* to portray this battle).

2. When using storytelling to illustrate or present events from other subject areas, supplement the storytelling with video, films, or subsequent discussions of the pictures in the subject textbook. Ask about any differences students may have noted between the teacher's story and the pictures in the text.

3. Have students tell stories of various types—stories that really happened or makeup stories—to illustrate concepts. In a lesson on gravity, the teacher may say something like, "Who can tell a funny story from your family about when something fell?"

4. Have several children retell the same story, movie, or television show. Explore with the class the differences in each child's version, without making any student "wrong" or "right."

5. In the middle of stories, stop to check on children's understanding of the narrative. Teachers may use questions such as, "Who can tell me what may happen next?" or "Who can tell me what Tabitha really wants to happen?"

6. Have children use physical movement in telling stories to the class. Have one student tell a story while several other students silently "act out" the story for the class. Use those actors to discuss how emotions may be portrayed or to discuss the feelings of the actors.

7. Use music, rhythms, or chants to tell stories. Some stories involve repeated lines or phrases, and these can be done as a chant by the entire class as the teacher tells the story. This will increase the attention of students with learning disabilities since they will be listening for the opportunity to participate in the chant.

8. Have the students discuss and subsequently demonstrate how they might tell the same story to different groups. For example, telling a story to students at a lower grade level would involve telling the story differently from telling the same story to one's parents or other adults. Students should reflect on what different terms or examples may be used.

9. Expose different students to different parts of the same story and let each student tell his or her part in sequence. Use a video and this same idea, and after each student has contributed his or her part, show the video to the class. Discuss what aspects of the story were omitted, if any.

10. Use drama and role-play to illustrate stories as the teacher tells them. Allow students to sense or feel the roles of the characters in the story.

8

What's Next?

Strategies Included in This Chapter:

✔ Self-Evaluation for Differentiated Instruction

✔ Targeting Students in Need

✔ Initiating Action Research

✔ Developing a Professional Improvement Plan

Having explored the strategies and tactics presented in the first seven chapters, teachers may need some suggestions for beginning the process of differentiated instruction in their class. This final chapter is designed to present teachers with some suggestions about how to proceed into this new and challenging way of teaching. This chapter is not intended as a "blueprint" for instructional change because most veteran teachers do not need such a cookbook approach. Also, many veteran teachers may have already incorporated many of these strategies and ideas into their typical classroom routine. Still, teachers may want some ideas on how to proceed. Below are some suggestions for improving instruction using the differentiated instruction model in the inclusive class for students with learning disabilities.

SELF-EVALUATION AND SELF-CONGRATULATIONS

As a first step in this process, teachers should consider the strategies and tactics that are already in use and congratulate themselves for already using some of these ideas. Although the term *differentiated instruction* is new, many of the strategies and tactics that are applied in the differentiated instructional classroom are not, and teachers already may be doing many of these things. For example, the emphasis on authentic assessment and portfolio assessment has been noted for the past ten years or so, and many teachers are evaluating students using a variety of diverse approaches. Likewise, the self-monitoring strategy is not new, and with decades of research attesting to its efficacy, many teachers are using that strategy already.

When undertaking significant change in one's teaching procedures, it is always wise to find reason for self-praise, and a brief summation of the strategies and tactics that one already employs will allow almost every teacher a reason for pride in his or her teaching. Consequently, one of the most important things teachers can do when exploring a new approach is to consciously identify reasons for pride in their current work. Although this text does recommend many adaptations in teachers' instructional efforts, these should be interpreted as ideas to improve a successful instructional technique and not to rebuild a failing career. The teachers that I work with (and I work with thousands each year) are by and large highly skilled professionals who are motivated to seek out enriching modifications for their classroom technique. In that sense, the strategies herein can assist those teachers.

📖 REFLECTIVE EXERCISE: SELF-EVALUATION AND SELF-CONGRATULATIONS

As a first step, teachers should print out the Bender Classroom Structure Questionnaire (BCSQ) (from Chapter 1) and each of the "ten tactics" lists from the various chapters. With those forms and lists as a guide, teachers should conduct an honest appraisal of how many of those strategies are currently in use in the classroom. In fact, the brief rating procedure below can help teachers determine what tactics to emphasize first. Teachers may do this by asking three questions.

1. What strategies and tactics are already implemented? These tactics are implemented already and not included in the rating.

2. Which strategies would be fairly easy to implement next, based on your teaching style and current procedures? Teachers should rate each indicator on this scale, with a 1 for *very difficult to implement*, 2 for *somewhat difficult to implement*, and 3 for *fairly easy to implement, given my current instructional approaches*.

3. What strategies would make the most positive instructional difference for the individual learners in your class? Teachers should rate each indicator on this question with 1 for *makes only a little difference*, 2 for *makes some difference for some students*, or 3 for *makes an important difference for many learners in my class*. For each indicator, merely multiply the ratings for questions 2 and 3 above,

and the higher indicators indicate the types of strategies teachers should implement first in the move toward a differentiated classroom.

After the self-evaluation and self-congratulations, teachers may wish to identify one or two of the strategies presented in this self-evaluation and try them! For example, teachers are often motivated to attempt a new strategy because another teacher in the building has tried the strategy and had success with it. Alternatively, teachers sometimes hear of innovative ideas at conferences or learn of new ideas from reading educational journals and then apply those in their own class. Many teachers implement strategies based on a desire to "try something new." There is certainly nothing wrong with this effort at modifying one's teaching style, and there is no time like the present to select several of these strategies and apply them.

TARGETING STUDENTS IN NEED

Of course, when choosing to move toward a more differentiated classroom, targeting strategies for specific students would seem to be most effective. By targeting students first in the change process, teachers are more likely to make a qualitative difference in the lives of their students and, ultimately, in their own enjoyment of teaching. Thus, I recommend targeting one's efforts at instructional modification to specific needs of specific students.

After some reflection on what strategies and tactics are already in use, teachers should consider their relationships to particular students as well as the learning endeavors of those students. Are there students who do not seem to be "making it" on most class activities? Teachers should envision the most recent instructional problems they noted for those students. Perhaps some students seem to need more support in comprehension of their reading assignments. Perhaps other students need assistance in developing self-regulatory skills for organizing their homework assignments. Again, teachers should think of the specific needs of the students and identify those students who need the most assistance. Specifically, teachers must think in terms of one or two specific problems demonstrated with some frequency by particular students and then determine the relative importance of those problems.

REFLECTIVE EXERCISE: STUDENTS IN NEED

What three students are in the most trouble academically in the class? Are there similarities in their learning processes that the teacher can identify (e.g., a tactile learner, or a learner who needs numerous concrete examples; a learner who needs movement built into the lesson, or a learner who needs to demonstrate his or her competency by a project, performance, or portfolio)? How do these students' problems manifest themselves in the classroom? What subject areas and what types of academic exercises are most indicative of the problems? Write a paragraph about each of the three students, noting these specific needs.

INITIATING ACTION RESEARCH

Action research is classroom-based research undertaken by teachers to solve specific learning problems demonstrated by particular students. The first two sections of this chapter involved consideration of the teacher's classroom organization and instructional strategies that were currently in use, as well as the needs of particular students who may be having trouble. With those considerations in mind, teachers are ready to plan and initiate an intervention project to differentiate the learning in their class for those students in need. In conducting this type of action research project, teachers move through a five-step process, including the following:

1. Isolate a learning problem of a particular student (describe the learning problem in detail).

2. Select an intervention for that problem and that student (after review of an array of strategies, select a strategy that has proven effectiveness and that the teacher believes may work for that student).

3. State an action research hypothesis and implement the strategy (e.g., the self-management strategy will help this student be prepared for class).

4. Take data to evaluate the effectiveness of the intervention (complete an action research intervention with a minimum of three weeks of data).

5. Evaluate the action research. (Did the intervention work? Is it necessary to continue? What other strategies might work if the first strategy did not?)

Using these five steps, teachers can select any of the differentiated instructional strategies in this text and implement an intervention. Teaching Tip 8.1 provides a brief form that may be of assistance in considering the problems as well as the possible interventions. However,

☞ Teaching Tip 8.1

Identifying a Student's Learning Problem

Student's Name _____ Date _____

1. Describe the most recent academic difficulty this student displayed. _____

   _____

2. What type of educational activity was the student doing? _____

   _____

3. Was this a problem in motivation (i.e., student not attempting the work) or in the
   learning process itself?_____

   _____

4. Does the activity the student was attempting lend itself to a particular strategy
   described here? _____

   _____

5. Can specialized strategies such as peer tutoring, authentic assessment, or self-
   management help? _____

   _____

6. Can the teacher state a hypothesis about a particular activity that may work for
   this student to alleviate this type of problem on similar tasks in the future? _____

   _____

With this information teachers should undertake an action research project to
determine if the strategy or strategies selected above can alleviate the problem for this
struggling student.

teachers should realize that almost any of the evaluation activities in this book may be of use here also.

A PROFESSIONAL IMPROVEMENT PLAN

Teachers, like all professionals, are expected to remain constantly updated in their profession, and although the demands on the teachers' time are many and varied, almost all teachers strive to constantly improve their instructional efforts. Thus, teachers

- Read professional journals
- Take college courses for professional recertification
- Attend conferences where innovative instructional ideas are presented
- Talk with other veteran teachers about problems that students are having and teaching strategies that may alleviate those problems
- Reflect on their instructional efforts constantly, in an effort to constantly improve

A professional improvement plan is one step that teachers can take to pull together these various activities and give some cohesion to these diverse professional development efforts. As teachers move to a differentiated classroom, the development and use of a professional improvement plan may help. Teaching Tip 8.2 presents a simple professional improvement plan that may serve as a model for teachers who wish to develop a differentiated instructional inclusive classroom.

CONCLUSION

With the strategies described herein, coupled with a continual effort to improve one's teaching, a differentiated classroom is within reach of every professional educator today. Not only will one become a more effective teacher, but students with learning disabilities will also benefit much more from the individual instruction that characterizes the differentiated classroom, and this will improve the relationship between the students and the teacher. In turn, by developing a differentiated instruction classroom, teachers typically find that they enjoy their teaching, and their students, even more. In this fashion, all teachers can more concretely enhance the learning and, ultimately, the lives of the students with learning disabilities in their classes, and these students deserve nothing less than the best we educators can offer.

☞ Teaching Tip 8.2

A Professional Improvement Plan

Name _____ Date _____

School _____

Proposed Professional Development Activities for Academic Year:

_____

I. Professional Knowledge Activities

1. I will read a minimum of fifteen journal articles on differentiated instruction and create an annotated bibliography on those articles.

2. I will attend one state conference and seek out sessions on differentiated instruction.

3. I will read two books on differentiated instruction and develop a one-page synopsis on each to share with the faculty at my school.

4. I will create a portfolio over the course of the year to synthesize all of these activities.

II. Action Research

1. I will develop two action research projects with two different students between September and December of next year.

2. I will present the results of those action research projects to the principal in January of the following year.

III. Professional Engagement

1. I will make a forty-five-minute presentation to our school faculty on differentiated instruction in the spring of next year.

2. I will submit a proposal to present my action research to a state meeting of the _____ (name of the teacher's professional organization here).

References

Arreaga-Mayer, C. (1998). Increasing active student responding and improving academic performance through classwide peer tutoring. *Intervention in School and Clinic, 24*(2), 89-117.

Ashton, T. M. (1999). Spell CHECKing: Making writing meaningful in the classroom. *Teaching Exceptional Children, 32*(2), 24-27.

Ausubel, D. P., & Robinson, F. G. (1969). *School learning: An introduction to educational psychology.* New York: Holt, Reinhart, & Winston.

Baumann, J. F. (1984). The effectiveness of a direct instruction paradigm for teaching main idea comprehension. *Reading Research Quarterly, 20,* 93-115.

Baumann, J. F. (1986). Teaching third-grade students to comprehend anaphoric relationships: The application of a direct instruction model. *Reading Research Quarterly, 21,* 70-87.

Beirne-Smith, M. (1991). Peer tutoring in arithmetic for children with learning disabilities. *Exceptional Children, 57,* 330-337.

Bender, W. N. (1985). Strategies for helping the mainstreamed student in secondary social studies classes. *Social Studies, 76,* 269-271.

Bender, W. N. (1986). Effective practices in the mainstream setting: Recommended model for evaluation of mainstream teachers' classes. *Journal of Special Education, 20,* 475-487.

Bender, W. N. (1992). The Bender classroom structure questionnaire: A tool for placement decisions and evaluation of mainstream learning environments. *Intervention in School and Clinic, 27,* 307-312.

Bender, W. N. (1996). *Teaching students with mild disabilities.* Boston: Allyn & Bacon.

Bender, W. N. (2002). *Relational discipline: Strategies for in-your-face kids.* Needham Heights, MA: Allyn & Bacon.

Bender, W. N., & Beckoff, A. G. (1989). Programming for mainstream kindergarten success in preschool: Teachers' perceptions of necessary prerequisite skills. *Journal of Early Intervention, 13*(3), 269-280.

Bender, W. N., Smith, J. K., & Frank, J. N. (1988). Evaluation of mainstream classes: A scale for determining appropriate class placements. *Education, 108,* 540-545.

Bender, W. N., & Ukeje, I. C. (1989). Instructional strategies in mainstream classrooms: Prediction of the strategies teachers select. *Remedial and Special Education, 10*(2), 22-30.

Bender, W. N., Vail, C. O., & Scott, K. (1995). Teachers' attitudes toward increased mainstreaming: Implementing effective instruction for students with learning disabilities. *Journal of Learning Disabilities, 28*(2), 87-94.

Bergerud, D., Lovitt, T. C., & Horton, S. (1988). The effectiveness of textbook adaptations in life science for high school students with learning disabilities. *Journal of Learning Disabilities, 21,* 70-76.

Bos, C. S., Mather, N., Silver-Pacuilla, H., & Narr, R. F. (2000). Learning to teach early literacy skills—collaboratively. *Teaching Exceptional Children, 32*(5), 38-45.

Brown, A. L., & Palincsar, A. S. (1982). Inducing strategic learning from texts by means of informed self-control training. *Topics in Learning and Learning Disabilities, 2*(2), 1-17.

Bryant, B. R. (1999). The dynamics of assessment. In W. N. Bender (Ed.), *Professional issues in learning disabilities* (pp. 253-279). Austin, TX: PRO-ED.

Bryant, D. P., Ugel, N., Thompson, S., & Hamff, A. (1999). Instructional strategies for content-area reading instruction. *Intervention in School and Clinic, 34*(5), 293-302.

Carlson, M. B., Litton, F. W., & Zinkgraf, S. A. (1985). The effects of an intraclass peer tutoring program on the sight word recognition ability of students who are mildly mentally retarded. *Mental Retardation, 23*(2), 74-78.

Carman, R. A., & Adams, W. R. (1972). *Study skills: A student's guide for survival.* New York: John Wiley.

Chapman, C. (2000, March 16). *Brain compatible instruction.* Paper presented at a nationwide telesatellite workshop, *Tactics for Brain Compatible Instruction,* Bishop, GA.

Chard, D. J., & Dickson, S. V. (1999). Phonological awareness: Instructional and assessment guidelines. *Intervention in School and Clinic, 34*(5), 261-270.

Clark, F. L., Deshler, D. D., Schumaker, J. B., Alley, G. R., & Warner, M. M. (1984). Visual imagery and self-questioning: Strategies to improve comprehension of written material. *Journal of Learning Disabilities, 17,* 145-149.

Corry, J. R., & Shamow, J. (1972). The effects of fading on the acquisition and retention of oral reading. *Journal of Applied Behavior Analysis*, 5, 311-315.

Cowan, G., & Cowan, E. (1980). *Writing.* New York: John Wiley.

Craig, S., Hull, K., Haggart, A. G., & Crowder, E. (2001). Storytelling: Addressing the literacy needs of diverse learners. *Teaching Exceptional Children, 33*(5), 46-52.

Darch, C., & Carnine, D. (1986). Teaching content area material to learning disabled students. *Exceptional Children, 53*, 240-246.

Darch, C., & Gersten, R. (1986). Direction-setting activities in reading comprehension: A comparison of two approaches. *Learning Disability Quarterly, 9,* 235-243.

Darch, C., & Kameenui, E. J. (1987). Teaching LD students critical reading skills: A systematic replication. *Learning Disability Quarterly, 10, 82-91.*

Day, V. P., & Elksnin, L. K. (1994). Promoting strategic learning. *Intervention in School and Clinic, 29*(5), 262-270.

Dayton-Sakari, M. (1997). Struggling readers don't work at reading: They just get their teachers to! *Intervention in School and Clinic, 32*(5), 295-301.

Delquadri, J., Greenwood, C. R., Whorton, D., Carta, J. J., & Hall, R. V. (1986). Classwide peer tutoring. *Exceptional Children, 52*, 535-542.

Deshler, D. D., Warner, M.. M., Schumaker, J. B., & Alley, G. R. (1984). Learning strategies intervention model: Key components and current status. In J. D. McKinney & L. Feagans (Eds.), *Current topics in learning disabilities* (Vol. 1). Norwood, NJ: Ablex.

Dickson, S. V., Chard, D. J., & Simmons, D. C. (1993). An integrated reading/writing curriculum: A focus on scaffolding. *LD Forum, 18*(4), 12-16.

Digangi, S., & Magg, J., & Rutherford, R. B. (1991). Self-graphing on on-task behavior: Enhancing the reactive effects of self-monitoring on-task behavior and academic performance. *Learning Disability Quarterly, 14*, 221-229.

Dorry, G. W. (1976). Attentional model for the effectiveness of fading in training reading-vocabulary with retarded persons. *American Journal of Mental Deficiency*, 81, 271-279.

Dye, G. A. (2000). Graphic organizers to the rescue! *Teaching Exceptional Children, 33*(4), 72-76.

Elbaum, B., Moody, S. W., Vaughn, S., Schumm, J. S., & Hughes, M. (2000). *The effect of instructional grouping format on the reading outcomes of students with disabilities: A meta-analytic review* [Online]. Available: www.ncld.org.

Ellis, E. S. (1994). Integrating writing strategy instruction with content area instruction. *Intervention in School and Clinic, 29,* 169-179.

Ellis, E. S., Deshler, D. D., & Schumaker, J. B. (1989). Teaching adolescents with learning disabilities to generate and use task-specific strategies. *Journal of Learning Disabilities, 22,* 108-118.

Engelmann, S., & Carnine, D. W. (1972). *DISTAR Arithmetic III.* Chicago: Scientific Research Associates.

Engelmann, S., & Hanner, S. (1982). *Reading Mastery, Level III: A direct instruction program.* Chicago: Science Research Associates.

Engelmann, S., Osborn, S., & Hanner, S. (1989). *Corrective reading: Comprehension skills comprehension B 2.* Chicago: Science Research Associates.

Englert, C. S., Berry, R., & Dunsmore, K. (2001). A case study of the apprenticeship process: Another perspective on the apprentice and the scaffolding metaphor. *Journal of Learning Disabilities, 34*(2), 152-171.

Fuchs, L. S., & Deno, S. L. (1994). Must instructionally useful performance assessment be based in the curriculum? *Exceptional Children, 61,* 15-24.

Fuchs, L. S., Fuchs, D., Eaton, S. B., Hamlett, C., Binkley, E., & Crouch, R. (2000). Using objective data sources to enhance teacher judgements about test accommodations. *Exceptional Children, 67*(1), 67-81.

Fuchs, L. S., Fuchs, D., Hamlett, C. L., Phillips, N. B., & Bentz, J. (1994). Classwide curriculum-based measurement: Helping general educators meet the challenge of student diversity. *Exceptional Children, 60,* 518-537.

Fuchs, L. S., Fuchs, D., Hamlett, C. C., Phillips, N. B., & Bentz, J. (1995). General educators' specialized adaptation for students with disabilities. *Exceptional Children, 61,* 440-459.

Fuchs, L. S., Fuchs, D., & Kazdan, S. (1999). Effects of peer-assisted learning strategies on high school students with serious reading problems. *Remedial and Special Education, 20*(5), 309-318.

Fuchs D., Fuchs, L., Yen, L., McMaster, K., Svenson, E., Yang, N., Young, C., Morgan, P., Gilbert, T., Jaspers, J., Jernigan, M., Yoon, E., & King, S. (2001). Developing first grade reading fluency through peer mediation. *Teaching Exceptional Children, 34*(2), 90-93.

Fulk, B. M., & King, K. (2001). Classwide peer tutoring at work. *Teaching Exceptional Children, 34*(2), 49-53.

Gersten, R., Woodward, J., & Darch, C. (1986). Direct instruction: A research-based approach to curriculum design and teaching. *Exceptional Children, 53,* 17-31.

Greenwood, C. R. (1991). Longitudinal analysis of time, engagement, and achievement in at-risk versus non-risk students. *Exceptional Children, 50,* 521-535.

Greenwood, C. R., Delquadri, J. C., & Hall, R. V. (1989). Longitudinal effects of classwide peer tutoring. *Journal of Educational Psychology, 81*(3), 371-383.

Gregory, G. H., & Chapman, C. (2002). *Differentiated instructional strategies: One size doesn't fit all.* Thousand Oaks, CA: Corwin Press.

Hallahan, D. P., & Lloyd, J. W. (1987). A reply to Snider. *Learning Disability Quarterly, 10,* 299-306.

Hallahan, D. P., Lloyd, J. W., Kosiewicz, M. M., Kauffman, J. M., & Graves, A. W. (1979). Self-monitoring of attention as a treatment for a learning disabled boy's off-task behavior. *Learning Disability Quarterly, 2,* 24-32.

Hallahan, D. P., Lloyd, J. W., & Stoller, L. (1982). *Improving attention with self-monitoring: A manual for teachers.* Charlottesville: University of Virginia.

Hallahan, D. P., Marshall, K. J., & Lloyd, J. W. (1981). Self-recording during group instruction: Effects on attention to task. *Learning Disability Quarterly, 4,* 407-413.

Hallahan, D. P., & Sapona, R. (1983). Self-monitoring of attention with learning disabled children: Past research and current issues. *Journal of Learning Disabilities, 16,* 616-620.

Hewett, F. (1967). Educational engineering with emotionally disturbed children. *Exceptional Children, 33,* 459-467.

Jones, C. J. (2001a). CBAs that work: Assessing students' math content-reading levels. *Teaching Exceptional Children, 34*(1), 24-29.

Jones, C. A. (2001b). Teacher-friendly curriculum-based assessment in spelling. *Teaching Exceptional Children, 34*(2), 32-38.

Joseph, J., Noble, K., & Eden, G. (2001). The neurobiological basis of reading. *Journal of Learning Disabilities, 34*(6), 566-579.

Kameenui, E. J., Carnine, D. W., Darch, C. B., & Stein, M. (1986). Two approaches to the development phase of mathematics instruction. *Elementary School Journal, 5,* 633-650.

Kameenui, E. J., Carnine, D. W., Dixon, R. C., Simmons, D. C., & Coyne, M. D. (2002). *Effective teaching strategies that accommodate diverse learners* (2nd ed.). Upper Saddle River, NJ: Prentice Hall.

Keeler, M. L., & Swanson, H. L. (2001). Does strategy knowledge influence working memory in children with mathematical disabilities? *Journal of Learning Disabilities, 34,* 418-434.

Knowlton, H. E. (1980). Effects of picture fading on two learning disabled students' sight word acquisition. *Learning Disability Quarterly, 3,* 88-96.

Korinek, L., & Bulls, J. A. (1996). SCORE A: A student research paper writing strategy. *Teaching Exceptional Children, 28*(4), 60-63.

Kuder, S. J. (1990). Effectiveness of the DISTAR Reading Program for children with learning disabilities. *Journal of Learning Disabilities, 23,* 69-71.

Larkin, M. J. (2001). Providing support for student independence through scaffolded instruction. *Teaching Exceptional Children, 34*(1), 30-35.

Lazerson, D. B., Foster, H. L., Brown, S. I., & Hummel, J. (1988). The effectiveness of cross-age tutoring with truant, junior high school students with learning disabilities. *Journal of Learning Disabilities, 21,* 253-255.

Lederer, J. M. (2000). Reciprocal teaching of social studies in inclusive elementary classrooms. *Journal of Learning Disabilities, 33*(1), 91-106.

Lenz, B. K., Alley, G. R., & Schumaker, J. B. (1987). Activating the inactive learner: Advance organizers in the secondary classroom. *Learning Disability Quarterly, 10,* 53-67.

Lenz, B. K., & Hughes, C. A. (1990). A word identification strategy for adolescents with learning disabilities. *Journal of Learning Disabilities, 23,* 149-163.

Lenz, B. K., Schumaker, J. B., Deshler, D. D., & Beals, V. L. (1984). *The word identification strategies* (Learning Strategies Curriculum). Lawrence: University of Kansas Press.

Leonard, C. M. (2001). Imaging brain structure in children: Differentiating language disability and reading disability. *Learning Disability Quarterly, 24*(3), 158-176.

Lindsley, O. R. (1971). Precision teaching in perspective: An interview with Ogden R. Lindsley (A. Duncan, interviewer). *Teaching Exceptional Children, 3,* 114-119.

Linn, R. L. (1986). Educational testing and assessment: Research needs and policy issues. *American Psychologist, 41,* 1153-1160.

Lovitt, T., & Horton, S. V. (1994). Strategies for adapting science textbooks for youth with learning disabilities. *Remedial and Special Education, 15*(2), 105-116.

Lovitt, T., Rudsit, J., Jenkins, J., Pious, C., & Benedetti, D. (1985). Two methods of adapting science materials for learning disabled and regular seventh graders. *Learning Disability Quarterly, 8,* 275-285.

Lyon, G. R., & Moats, L. C. (1997). Critical conceptual and methodological considerations in reading intervention research. *Journal of Learning Disabilities, 30*(6), 578-588.

Maheady, L., Harper, G. F., & Sacca, K. (1988). A classwide peer tutoring system in a secondary, resource room program for the mild handicapped. *Journal of Research and Development in Education, 21*(3), 76-83.

Maher, C. A. (1982). Behavioral effects of using conduct problem adolescents as cross-age tutors. *Psychology in the Schools, 19,* 360-364.

Maher, C. A. (1984). Handicapped adolescents as cross age tutors: Program description and evaluation. *Exceptional Children, 51,* 56-63.

Marks, J. W., Laeys, J. V., Bender, W. N., & Scott, K. S. (1996). Teachers create learning strategies: Guidelines for classroom creation. *Teaching Exceptional Children, 28*(4), 34-38.

Marston, D., Tindal, G., & Deno, S. L. (1984). Eligibility for learning disabilities services: A direct and repeated measurement approach. *Exceptional Children, 50,* 554-556.

Mastropieri, M. A., Leinart, A., & Scruggs, T. E. (1999). Strategies to increase reading fluency. *Intervention in School and Clinic, 34*(5), 278-283.

Mastropieri, M. A., & Peters, E. E. (1987). Increasing prose recall of learning disabled and reading disabled students via spatial organizers. *Journal of Educational Research, 80,* 272-276.

Mastropieri, M. A., & Scruggs, T. E. (1988). Increasing content area learning of learning disabled students: Research implementation. *Learning Disabilities Research, 4*(1), 17-25.

Mastropieri, M. A., & Scruggs, T. E. (1998). Enhancing school success with mnemonic strategies. *Intervention in School and Clinic, 33*(4), 201-208.

Mathes, M., & Bender, W. N. (1997a). The effects of self-monitoring on children with attention-deficit/hyperactivity disorder who are receiving pharmacological interventions. *Remedial and Special Education, 18*(2), 121-128.

Mathes, M., & Bender, W. N. (1997b). Teaching students with ADHD in the elementary classroom: A hierarchical approach to strategy selection. In W. N. Bender (Ed.), *Understanding ADHD: A practical guide for teachers and parents.* Columbus, OH: Charles Merrill.

Mathes, P. G., Fuchs, D., Fuchs, L. S., & Henley, A. M. (1994). Increasing strategic reading practice with Peabody classwide peer tutoring. *Learning Disabilities Research and Practice, 9*(1), 44-48.

Mathes, P. G., Fuchs, D., Roberts, P. H., & Fuchs, L. S. (1998). Preparing students with special needs for reintegration: Curriculum-based measurement's impact on transenvironmental programming. *Journal of Learning Disabilities, 31*(6), 615-624.

McConnell, M. E. (1999). Self-monitoring, cueing, recording, and managing: Teaching students to manage their own behavior. *Teaching Exceptional Children, 32*(2), 14-23.

McTighe, J. (1990). *Better thinking and learning.* Baltimore: Maryland State Department of Education.

Meichenbaum, D. H., & Goodman, J. (1969). The developmental control of operant motor responding by verbal operants. *Journal of Experimental Child Psychology, 7,* 553-565.

Meichenbaum, D. H., & Goodman, J. (1988). Training impulsive children to talk to themselves: A means of developing self-control. *Journal of Abnormal Psychology, 77,* 115-126.

Miller, M., & Fritz, M. F. (1998). A demonstration of resilience. *Intervention in School and Clinic, 35,* 265-271.

Moats, L. C., & Lyon, G. R. (1993). Learning disabilities in the United States: Advocacy, science, and the future of the field. *Journal of Learning Disabilities, 26,* 282-294.

Monda-Amoya, L., & Reed, F. (1993). Informal assessment in the classroom. In W. N. Bender (Ed.), *Best practices in learning disabilities* (pp. 105-134). Reading, MA: Andover Medical Publishers.

Montague, M. (1992). The effects of cognitive and metacognitive strategy instruction on the mathematical problem solving of middle school students with learning disabilities. *Journal of Learning Disabilities, 25,* 230-248.

Montague, M., & Leavell, A. G. (1994). Improving the narrative writing of students with learning disabilities. *Remedial and Special Education, 15*(1), 21-33.

Mortweet, S. W., Utley, C. A., Walker, D., Dawson, H. L., Delquardri, J. C., Reedy, S. S., Greenwood, C. R., Hamilton, S., & Ledford, D. (1999). Classwide peer tutoring: Teaching students with mild mental retardation in inclusive classrooms. *Exceptional Children, 65*(4), 524-536.

Palincsar, A. S., & Brown, A. L. (1986). Interactive teaching to promote independent learning from text. *The Reading Teacher, 39,* 771-777.

Palincsar, A. S., & Brown, A. L. (1987). Enhancing instructional time through attention to metacognition. *Journal of Learning Disabilities, 20*(1), 66-75.

Patzer, C. E., & Pettegrew, B. S. (1996). Finding a "voice": Primary students with developmental disabilities express personal meanings through writing. *Teaching Exceptional Children, 29*(2), 22-27.

Peterson, J., Heistad, D., Peterson, D., & Reynolds, M. (1985). Montevideo individualized prescriptive instructional management system. *Exceptional Children, 52,* 239-243.

Polloway, E. A., Epstein, M. H., Polloway, C. H., Patton, J. R., & Ball, D. W. (1986). Corrective reading program: An analysis of effectiveness with learning disabled and mentally retarded students. *Remedial and Special Education, 7*(4), 41-47.

Pressley, M., Hogan, K., Wharton-McDonald, R., Mistretta, J., & Ettneberger, S. (1996). The challenges of instructional scaffolding: The challenges of instruction that supports student thinking. *Learning Disabilities Research & Practice, 11*(3), 138-146.

Rabren, K., Darch, C., & Eaves, R. C. (1999). The differential effects of two systematic reading comprehension approaches with students with learning disabilities. *Journal of Learning Disabilities, 32*(1), 36-47.

Richards, T. L. (2001). Functional magnetic resonance imaging and spectroscopic imaging of the brain: Application of fMRI and fMRS to reading disabilities and education. *Learning Disability Quarterly, 24*(3), 189-204.

Rooney, K. J., & Hallahan, D. P. (1988). The effects of self-monitoring on adult behavior and student independence. *Learning Disabilities Research, 3*, 88-93.

Rooney, K. J., Hallahan, D. P., & Lloyd, J. W. (1984). Self-recording of attention by learning disabled students in the regular classroom. *Journal of Learning Disabilities, 17*, 360-363.

Rose, T. L., & Robinson, H. H. (1984). Effects of illustrations on learning disabled students' reading performance. *Learning Disability Quarterly, 7*, 165-171.

Russell, T., & Ford, D. F. (1984). Effectiveness of peer tutors vs. resource teachers. *Psychology in the Schools, 21*, 436-441.

Sasso, G. M., Mitchell, V. M., & Struthers, E. M. (1986). Peer tutoring vs. structured interaction activities: Effects on the frequency and topography of peer interactions. *Behavior Disorders, 11*, 249-258.

Scheid, K. (1994). Cognitive based methods for teaching mathematics. *Teaching Exceptional Children, 56*, 540-549.

Scruggs, T. E., Mastropieri, M., Veit, D. T., & Osguthorpe, R. G. (1986). Behaviorally disordered students as tutors: Effects on social behavior. *Behavior Disorders, 11*, 36-43.

Scruggs, T. E., & Richter, L. (1985). Tutoring learning disabled students: A critical review. *Learning Disability Quarterly, 8*, 286-298.

Shapiro, E. S., DuPaul, G. J., & Bradley-Klug, K. L. (1998). Self-management as a strategy to improve the classroom behavior of adolescents with ADHD. *Journal of Learning Disabilities, 31*(6), 545-555.

Smith, C. R. (1998). From gibberish to phonemic awareness: Effective decoding instruction. *Teaching Exceptional Children, 30*(6), 20-25.

Smith, S. B., Baker, S., & Oudeans, M. K. (2001). Making a difference in the classroom with early literacy instruction. *Teaching Exceptional Children, 33*(6), 8-14.

Snider, V. (1987). Use of self-monitoring of attention with LD students: Research and application. *Learning Disability Quarterly, 10,* 139-151.

Snyder, M. C., & Bambara, L. M. (1997). Teaching secondary students with learning disabilities to self-manage classroom survival skills. *Journal of Learning Disabilities, 30*(5), 534-543.

Sousa, D. (1999, April 23). *Motor learning in the classroom.* Paper presented at the teleconference, *Brain Based Learning,* Atlanta, GA.

Sousa, D. (2001a). *How the brain learns* (2nd ed.). Thousand Oaks, CA: Corwin Press.

Sousa, D. A. (2001b). *How the special needs brain learns.* Thousand Oaks, CA: Corwin Press.

Stone, C. A. (1998). The metaphor of scaffolding: Its utility for the field of learning disabilities. *Journal of Learning Disabilities, 31,* 344-364.

Swanson, P. N., & De La Paz, S. (1998). Teaching effective comprehension strategies to students with learning and reading disabilities. *Intervention in School and Clinic, 33*(4), 209-218.

Sylwester, R. (2000). *A biological brain in a cultural classroom.* Thousand Oaks, CA: Corwin Press.

Tomlinson, C. A. (1999). *The differentiated classroom: Responding to the needs of all learners.* Alexandria, VA: Association for Supervision and Curriculum Development.

Tomlinson, C. A. (2001). *How to differentiate instruction in mixed-ability classrooms* (2nd ed.). Alexandria, VA: Association for Supervision and Curriculum Development.

Tomlinson, C. A., Kaplan, S. N., Renzulli, J. S., Purcell, J., Leppien, J., & Burns, D. (2002). *The parallel curriculum: A design to develop high potential and challenge high-ability learners.* Thousand Oaks, CA: Corwin Press.

Top, B. L., & Osguthorpe, R. T. (1987). Reverse-role tutoring: The effects of handicapped students tutoring regular class students. *Elementary School Journal, 87,* 413-423.

Utley, C. A., Mortweet, S. L., & Greenwood, C. R. (1997). Peer-mediated instruction and interventions. *Focus on Exceptional Children, 29*(5), 1-23.

Vail, C. O., & Huntington, D. (1993). Classroom behavioral interventions for students with learning disabilities. In W. N. Bender (Ed.), *Best practices in learning disabilities* (pp. 153-176). Reading, MA: Andover Medical Publishers.

Vaughn, S., Gersten, R., & Chard, D. J. (2000). The underlying message in LD intervention research: Findings from research syntheses. *Exceptional Children, 67*(1), 99-114.

Wang, M. C., & Birch, J. W. (1984). Comparison of a full-time mainstreaming program and a resource room approach. *Exceptional Children, 51,* 33-40.

Wang, M. C., & Zollers, N. J. (1990). Adaptive instruction: An alternative service delivery approach. *Remedial and Special Education, 11*(1), 7-12.

Ward-Lonergan, J. M., Liles, B. Z., & Anderson, A. M. (1999). Verbal re-telling abilities in adolescents with and without language-learning disabilities for social studies lectures. *Journal of Learning Disabilities, 32*(3), 213-223.

Wesson, C. L. (1991). Curriculum based measurement and two models of follow-up consultation. *Exceptional Children, 57,* 246-256.

White, O. R. (1986). Precision teaching precision learning. *Exceptional Children, 52,* 522-534.

Winn, J. A., & Otis-Wilborn, A. (1999). Monitoring literacy learning. *Teaching Exceptional Children, 32*(1), 40-45.

Index